Sahib

Sahib

AN AMERICAN MISADVENTURE IN INDIA

BY CARL POPE

LIVERIGHT   NEW YORK

To Sri Ram Sewak Sinha
Block Extension Educator

Sahib

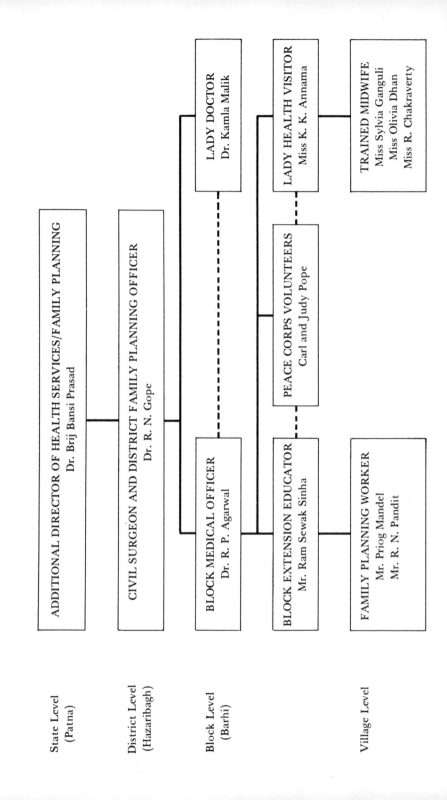

State Level
(Patna)

ADDITIONAL DIRECTOR OF HEALTH SERVICES/FAMILY PLANNING
Dr. Brij Bansi Prasad

District Level
(Hazaribagh)

CIVIL SURGEON AND DISTRICT FAMILY PLANNING OFFICER
Dr. R. N. Gope

Block Level
(Barhi)

LADY DOCTOR
Dr. Kamla Malik

BLOCK MEDICAL OFFICER
Dr. R. P. Agarwal

LADY HEALTH VISITOR
Miss K. K. Annama

PEACE CORPS VOLUNTEERS
Carl and Judy Pope

BLOCK EXTENSION EDUCATOR
Mr. Ram Sewak Sinha

Village Level

TRAINED MIDWIFE
Miss Sylvia Ganguli
Miss Olivia Dhan
Miss R. Chakraverty

FAMILY PLANNING WORKER
Mr. Priog Mandel
Mr. R. N. Pandit

1.

The unadorned concrete walls of the Delhi airport were lit with the grey-green light of low watt fluorescent bulbs. Outside it was dark, the air heavy with fog and smoke. A small bus waited to take us to the hotel. I waited for a sign of India. And then I realized that the street was not empty: a bullock cart driven by a man in a dark turban and white pajamas pulled out to pass the bus; a motor scooter wove its way between clumps of pedestrians; a horn honked somewhere down the road. The dust and the dark cut out all color and muted the sounds of the street. India met us in black and white.

For two days, between briefings and paper work at the American Embassy, we toured Delhi. I felt between my fingers the grainy flat wheat bread called chappati and savored its nutty taste. I watched government clerks hurry along the sidewalks in their sparkling white dhotis—they really did need one hand just to hold the pleats up! And to my surprise the taxi drivers did ask "Kaha janna he?" when they wanted to know where we were going, just as we had been taught they would.

When we set off with our Peace Corps colleagues for more instruction, at Rajgir, the air-conditioned car with its padded reclining seats and tinted glass put Penn Central to shame. I bought half a dozen oranges at a way station and spent an hour carefully peeling them with one hand. That way, the American doctor had told us, the other hand would be uncontaminated by germs on the skin of the orange. The Peace Corps had provided us with several large buckets of boiled water, but they sloshed around in the compartment and I was no longer confident. So

1

each time I filled a small paper cup with water, I added an iodine pill meant for a full pint and waited patiently while the water and the cup turned the color of grape juice. At each station the Indians got off the train and leaned under the faucets, drinking in great gulps of fresh cool water. My wife Judy and I and forty-three other Americans nursed our lukewarm cups of disinfectant. No amoeba or bacillus would interfere with our getting into the real India!

We left the train at Gaya, the station nearest the village of Rajgir where we would finish our training. Tommy Thomas, a tall, blond Volunteer from Texarkana who had been in the state of Bihar for eighteen months, met us on the platform. He shepherded us through a crowd of red-capped porters in white dhotis, past a row of cycle rickshaws, and pointed us toward a bus which had long since given up trying to sit level on its wheels. One door hinge was rusted through, the wooden floor was warped into ripples, and the seat cushions were only held in place by the weight of the passengers. We made our way forward.

There was no evening mist, no taxi windshield, no tinted train window between me and the town. Nothing in my university courses in economic development had prepared me for Gaya. The doctor in Delhi, warning us against uncooked food, had asked us to imagine that everything in India was covered wih a thin layer of human feces. In Gaya the layer seemed to be six inches thick. Manure piles, open sewers, flies, and rotten vegetable heaps competed for attention. "My God, why did I come?" was my first thought, followed by, "I don't think I can take it, but how can I leave without looking like a fool?"

Finally the sewers disappeared and were replaced by open fields. The manure piles now belonged. The bus came alive. "There's another bullock cart." "Look at the women harvesting that rice!" "What are those yellow flowers—mustard?" "My God, that taxi must have fifteen people in it!" "This is much nicer than Delhi."

An hour later we climbed out of the flat paddy lands and tilted over a rise. The sun was setting against a purple line of hills. Temples were outlined in black at each low peak. The road broke through a jagged stone wall.

Exhaustion replaced exhilaration as the bus pulled up at the yellow stucco training center. After dinner we stumbled off to bed, heads full of the impressions of the day.

We were scheduled for three weeks of "in-country" training in Rajgir. We gradually got to feel very in-country, but we received little training. No one from the language training staff in Lexington, Kentucky, had come out to supervise our first immersion in daily Hindi, and the lectures by government officials never touched on such questions as how to get the doctor sitting at the back of the room to sterilize his instruments. Still, we were sure that we knew how to find the answers; nothing threatened our self-confidence. We were responding to John Kennedy's appeal, only we were asking what we could do for Bihar. We had come to remake the family planning program.

We got down to basics. Three or four other veteran Volunteers joined Tommy in explaining the relative cost of beef, goat, and chicken; train reservations; the status of women; how to deal with servants. We admired their casual attitude toward eating bazaar food and drinking village water but we didn't accept it. Everything else they told us we accepted. It made for instant sophistication.

In the streets people addressed me as Sahib, and my wife Judy as Memsahib. College had taught me that colonial rule in India ended in 1947. But the British, it seemed, were still here. I was determined to escape that identification. People wanted to know who I was, and I needed an answer that would make sense in Rajgir and later in the village where we would work. If I was not an heir to the British Raj, I needed to adopt other ancestors, so I plunged into the local khadi shop.

Khadi is a handspun, handloomed cloth which Ghandi made the focus of his drive to restore the traditional village economy. He demanded of each freedom fighter a certain amount of thread spun each day. The government, once the first flush of Independence was over, permitted a heavy subsidy to keep the village spindles and looms going; but the Congress Party retained khadi as it's official uniform, and even Indira Ghandi wears only khadi silk.

I could not yet imitate Ghandi in the spinning of thread, but I could imitate his followers in wearing the cloth. In this way I would show my appreciation of Indian customs. When the light, loose-fitting shirt and pajamas were ready, I admired their look in the mirror and felt like an old hand. The cloth was comfortable, cool; it catered to a long desire of mine for clothing I didn't have to bother with. I liked its look on me and the fact that people in the street commented on it. I had one hesitation: I remembered from my summer as a civil rights worker in Arkansas the warning of the black project director that "some white kids try to out-sharecropper the sharecropper." Was I trying to outIndian Indians? No one in the streets seemed to think so.

Other Volunteers burned incense in their rooms, rose with the people of Rajgir at 6:00 A.M. and made the rounds of local shops for cups of tea and small talk which none of us could really follow. Judy and I tried in other ways to join India. When the food was overspiced we kept quiet, and we ate great gobs of peanut butter on bananas.

As long as all of us were together in Rajgir there was an escape. We would absorb as much as we could outside and then return to our small courtyard on the hill. Our room was bare concrete and lit by kerosene lanterns. I had to tuck in a mosquito net before I went to sleep. But the voices around me were American, and I knew that my curses at the ingenuity of the mosquito would be sympathetically heard. The back alleys remained *back* alleys; in the front of my consciousness was the training program with its familiar schedule and reassuring reliance on English. I could not get too deeply into Rajgir as a place different from other places in India. I was still dealing with abstractions, from which I would return to real life with the forty-four Volunteers of India 51.

After three weeks of training, the Peace Corps considered us ready for a trial run. So late one afternoon, Judy and I walked to the village of Bhui, introduced ourselves to Rajkumar Prasad, the mukhia or headman with whom were were to live for a week, sat down in front of his house and wondered what next. This was a family whose life we would share, in whose house we would sleep, and whose language and rules and village we must come to terms with. We would be uncomfortable, I knew, but then we would leave, return to Rajgir and rejoin our friends.

We sat on a woven string cot beneath an arbor of bamboo over which Rajkumar had trained a thick green vine bearing large yellow gourds. Behind us was a small pond, overhung by several great trees. A set of broad stairs ran from the water up to a small stucco temple. The steps were lined with laundry drying in the fading sun.

A dirt path ran between the arbor and the front of the house. The house was built of brick, with low doors and small windows. At each side a room opened directly to the front; the main entrance led back to the courtyard. Rajkumar supervised while several men cleared a mass of straw from one of the rooms opening onto the path. The room apparently served as a stable for goats. A large string cot was then juggled through the door and we were invited to unpack.

Six or seven family members gathered to watch while we unrolled our bedrolls. I had never thought of unpacking as a particularly private activity, but suddenly it was. Yet the comments from our observers were, without exception, favorable. Each item loosed a stream of eager questions. Once an article had been catalogued as to function, age, and price, Judy and I were allowed to place it on one of the shelves built into the brick. When we were through, one of Rajkumar's sons brought in a small table and it was time to eat.

We stepped outside to wash our hands, Judy pouring water for me out of the brass jug, I in turn helping her. The family watched and I wondered if I was doing it correctly. Then we went in. I had given up hope that we would eat in privacy and was worried about the highly spiced food. In Rajgir it had produced tears and runny noses. But Rajkumar assured us that he had warned "my women" against using too many chiles. Judy and I noted, in English, that the plates had been rinsed with unboiled water before they were handed to us. The doctor in Delhi had cautioned us about this custom but he had not told us what to do about it. We decided not to worry and hurried through the meal, which was good. After dinner we were still encircled by our watchers, but at least we could talk and look back at them.

We enjoyed the evenings in Bhui. As the sun set behind the pond, we sat under the trellis in heaps of straw, warming our hands over pots of hot ashes. The children, and there were over twenty of them in Rajkumar's extended family, gathered around the outside of the circle. Rajkumar brought out his radio, tuned in the news and talked to us over the flickering sound. The village leaders drifted in. We met the schoolteacher, the head of the local Muslim community, the agricultural extension worker. Between patient questions about agriculture, marriage, and money in America, they exchanged the day's gossip and discussed the outlook for the next day.

This was Judy's first crisis—only the men sat under the trellis. After dinner the first night she had gone back into the house to meet the women. Rajkumar still followed the custom of purdah, and I heard but never saw the wives who worked behind the blue curtain at the doorway to the courtyard. Once inside the house with the women, Judy found that she could not communicate. We had learned Hindustani, the lingua franca of North India. The local dialect was quite different. Hindustani is the language of merchants and traders; it was learned in the bazaar, so all the men knew it. We had not learned the speech of kitchens and bedrooms. Judy ended up silently watching the women prepare meals while they tried to explain to her what they were doing.

Eventually Judy did join me under the trellis and was accepted because she was a foreigner, a memsahib. They were even curious about her opinions. But a lifetime of segregation from women, of never conversing with them because they had nothing to say and were only women, was not easily laid aside. They talked to Judy through me. "Does Judy like wearing saris?" and she would reply, though not addressed, "They're very pretty, but I'm not very good at it yet."

Rajkumar was away during the day and we were free to wander. Bhui was small, surrounded by rice paddies and palm trees. Narrow paths led to several outlying clusters of houses. We walked out to one lone house in the midst of the fields, with a cattle shed and a threshing floor. We squatted at one edge of a round earthen circle and the peasant and his children squatted at the other. Where had we come from? We pointed over the field to Bhui and explained that we were staying there. The peasant shook his head. We might as well have come from the sky. Why had we come? We tried to explain the Peace Corps, but he wanted to know why we had come to see *him*. We said we were just wandering, trying to see what the life of the people was like. He told us the crops were bad, the rains had failed, and that life everywhere was much the same. We assured him that rice did, indeed, grow in America. He considered his point confirmed: it's all the same. Looking at the flat fields, the great white herons dipping toward the small river, the mud houses, I could not agree. I had learned more from observing his tools, his bullock,

6

and his clothing than from our conversation.

The next morning, wandering down a narrow lane, we stumbled across some children flying small paper kites. They stared; we stared back. An old man sitting against a fence called out, "Let the sahib fly the kite." One of the boys handed me the frail string wrapped round a stick. I took it cautiously. The kite was hanging about fifty feet up and about eighty feet away from me. As I took the string, the kite dipped slightly. I tugged back, trying to imitate the boys. It swooped up, then turned again. I had no idea how to manipulate it. Then I saw that the kite had no tail, and as I desperately tried to pull it toward me, it nosedived into the path. Well, I thought, at least I've shown them that Americans don't do everything better!

The kite's owner soon had it up again. He turned to me, holding the kite string for me to take. I bit my lip, watching. His hands did not seem to move; the kite hung in the wind, vibrating slightly. Surely I could manage it? I reached out, fingers grasping the thin thread. He released the stick. I stood there, frozen, for about three seconds. The kite dipped, as it had the first time. I hoped the wind would save me. The kite soared, turned, and headed straight for a tall tree—the only one in sight. Too late I pulled back. My jerk only insured that the wisp of green paper lodged in the very highest branch. I groaned. Judy laughed. There was no way to recover the kite and my stomach contracted. It was only a bit of tissue paper on twigs, but I had no idea how hard it had been for the boy to get it, how easy to replace. I didn't know if I was being silly or not. I looked around, hoping I could offer to pay, but thought better of it. The children had treated me as a guest and I had seen enough in Rajkumar's house to know that guests do not offer to pay in Bhui. Apologizing in my Hindi, which struck me as terribly clumsy, I made my way out of the cluster of children, who stood watching us wide-eyed until we turned a corner in the lane.

The final morning, while I packed, Judy vanished into the house for one last session with the women. When she emerged half an hour later she had a rather foolish grin on her face. Rajkumar, standing at my side, clapped his hands in appreciation. "Now she's a real Indian woman!" he proclaimed. The women had painted her fingernails and toenails a brilliant red. He asked me how Judy liked the painting, and Judy assured him that it was beautiful and the women had been very kind. I put in a few good words, shouldered my bedroll on my head Indian-style, and said goodbye to Rajkumar and the assembled children. As we walked towards Rajgir, I smiled at Judy. I knew she hated nail polish. Now she looked at me in exasperation. "I had to keep lying, I had to keep telling them how beautiful it is, how wonderful of them to do it; I feel like they steamrollered me. But they'd been trying to talk to me all week, and I just couldn't say no!"

We were glad to escape. I looked back. I could see the tree, but the green kite was hidden by dust.

In theory, during the remaining days in Rajgir we were supposed to discuss our week in the village; in fact, we settled back into our American world to quiet some of the fears and doubts that had been raised. Our last day in Rajgir would be the twenty-fourth of December, and since there were no evergreens in Rajgir, we picked a small, bare tree and whitewashed it as a Christmas tree. We used real candles, gathered masses of flowers, and strung red chile peppers in place of cranberries. We bought fireworks in the bazaar and had sparklers. As Christmas Eve approached, it came over us that our whitewashed branches were not white pine, that the Sanskrit chants we could hear from the temples were not carols, that we were far from home. We gathered around the tree at one end of a bare room and sang carols. Few of us knew the second or third verses of any. Before it had never mattered, now we felt deprived. When we had sung all we knew, we cast about for something else to hold off India: old rock and roll, folk songs, union or civil rights versions of the same folk songs, humorous takeoffs on folk songs, "America the Beautiful." We closed with "The Star-Spangled Banner," and were embarrassed. Remembering the training we had received in the States, we stood in rows and sang "Jana Gana Mana," the Indian national anthem. When we finished, one of the Volunteers looked at his watch. "Forty-five seconds. Too fast." Our instructors in Lexington had told us that the anthem should take fifty-one seconds exactly; it took that long to sing it at the opening of the Indian parliament.

The next morning we took down the white tree and tossed it into a ravine. Christmas whitewash mixed with red dust.

Judy and I were lucky. We were assigned to the site we requested, a village called Barhi in the southern hill district of Bihar, and on a bright December morning we left the protective hills of Rajgir and our Peace Corps friends.

At first the countryside unfolded in the pattern we had seen in Bhui—a foreground of flat fields in paddy green and mustard yellow, improbably set off by a background of brown hills which had no business combining so much steepness with so little height.

Barhi lay at an important junction on the road to Calcutta. We were traveling in a Peace Corps jeep and so we had the company of Amin, the Peace Corps driver, our last link with India 51. We asked Amin about various scenes as we passed. He must have told hundreds of fresh Volunteers the same things, but his eyes sparkled as he pointed out each change in the land. About two hours out of Rajgir we began to climb, and Amin told us we were about to enter the hill districts. The one-and-a-half-lane road twisted its way up into scrub forest. Soon the open slopes were dotted with unfamiliar trees. I recognized only bamboo. Amin told us that these were teak and mango, tamarind and guava. The names were familiar, but I could not fit the spice and aroma of the names with this dusty reality; although I had read about drought, I had expected India to be lush and tropical. Even a month in Rajgir had not prepared me for the fact that what Amin called jungle looked more like West Texas than the Amazon rain forest.

The open country was a relief; man did not press down as hard on this land. But I wondered where people lived. To teach family planning, we did not need the kind of crowding we had seen in Gaya, but we did need families!

The question was soon answered; in twenty minutes we reached the top of the slope and passed over the Chota Nagpur Plateau. Now the land had more form, a series of ridges and scrub woods trailed along the top of gentle slopes which had in many places been contoured like a map by paddy terraces. We passed Jhumri Tilaiya, one of the market towns used by the people of Barhi, and its railway center. It looked much like Rajgir or Gaya, but the buildings were set back ten yards or so from the road. There was more space.

Beyond Jhumri Tilaiya were the flat surfaces of an artificial reservoir, the first body of water we had seen in India; then the road looped over one of the ridges and we nosed our way into Barhi.

The scene was dominated by two major highways which intersected in the middle of the bazaar. A round concrete island in the center of the junction bore a yellow sign which warned: "Dead slow." The roadway was lined with shops and stalls built of warped lumber, flattened kerosene tins, and red clay tile, like those in Rajgir. Along the sides of the road six or seven old women guarded open baskets filled with fish, tomatoes, and onions. The town gave way to fields and then to hills. It would be nice to have a view.

We had reserved a room in the bungalow, the Indian equivalent of a motel. A wrought iron gate spanned the driveway leading to the low yellow building. We drove up under a latticed overhang draped with purple and pink bougainvillea; the red concrete steps to the veranda were crowded with tropical plants; and from the veranda we could see mango trees and the fields beyond. The order, the neatness, the foliage set the bungalow off from the town, even though the physical division was only a low brick wall over which goats jumped.

The manager showed us our room, which was spare but clean with a concrete bath attached. We hauled in our trunks, fitted our own combination lock in place of the heavy iron padlock that dangled from the door ring, and came out to say goodbye to Amin. I knew there were a hundred questions I should ask him, but I didn't know how to begin. So I said nothing, while he talked briefly with the manager—a conversation we could not follow, since it was not pitched to our speed and vocabulary. Then Amin got in the jeep, made the ritual gesture of namaste with folded palms, and drove off waving. Our hearts sank. The manager asked if we wanted anything; we told him no and went back to our room and sat on the canvas bed. The afternoon sunshine seemed chilly. I was sure only that I did not want to start out by trying to do anything; there was too much to learn first. But it was not easy to begin learning things. Sitting on the other end of the bed, Judy smiled at me. "Well?"

"Let's go look around," I said in Hindi. "There's nothing here."

She laughed. "It's our first wedding anniversary. And we

both forgot."

We set off in search of the doctor who would be supervising our work in family planning but found instead the Lady Doctor who would be working with Judy on supervising the female family planning staff. With her was the Block Development Officer, chief administrative official for Barhi and the hundred smaller villages that comprised Barhi Block or Township. They were drinking tea and got up to greet us.

Dr. Usha Narayin was tall, had elegant carriage, a wide mouth, and hands that never rested. She talked excellent staccato English and laughed at her own vitality. She invited all of us to dinner.

Mr. Kumar, the Development Officer, was a round-faced Christian from the western part of the state. Impeccably dressed in clean white pajamas, he wore three or four rings which he twisted to emphasize a point. Although he spoke good English, he seemed uncomfortable in the language, and Dr. Narayin stopped frequently to translate our idioms.

They both wanted to know exactly what we were going to do. What was our strategy for work? What was our schedule? Where would we go? Would we have a jeep?

I winced. The assumption that we might have a jeep spoke of the high status and wealth associated with white skins, which was not what we wanted. We went to great pains to explain that we would have no jeep but would travel by bicycle. And we emphasized that until we learned much more we could not know exactly how we would work. I had no idea of how to proceed and would have been glad for suggestions.

The main problem, as Dr. Narayin and Mr. Kumar outlined it, was that the staff did not work; they were lazy and unmotivated. Even so, the program had gone well until Dr. Agarwal left. Dr. Agarwal, we knew, was the chief doctor for the block; he had performed more male sterilizations in the previous year than any other doctor in the state. But now he was in Calcutta where his young son was undergoing medical treatment for a serious liver disease. For the moment Dr. Narayin was in charge. But in a week she would be leaving Barhi for a new position in a hospital. And the Extension Educator, the man who had worked under Dr. Agarwal on the education program and who was to be my official co-worker, had resigned.

"But his resignation has not been accepted, and until it is no one can be sent in his place."

I sighed and looked at Judy. We had been carefully coached on the importance of supplementing, not replacing, the existing structure. We were supposed to work within the chain of command in the block, to provide training for the staff, and to organize the work. But the key pieces, all of them, were missing from the board. Only the lowest level of staff was present in Barhi.

Well, I thought, while we tried to find a solution to the staff problem, we would need to organize our private lives as well.

Mr. Kumar had been thinking along the same lines. "You'll need a cook, won't you?"

We had had it drummed into us in training that the average Bihari's worst enemy was his diet, which left him without the animal vitality needed to cope with his life. We had no intention of embracing this low-protein life style and had been told that the only alternative was to have a cook. Volunteers in India had cooks. Yes, we wanted a cook, once we found a place to live.

"Well," said Mr. Kumar, "you can take Jagdish, the boy who cooks for Dr. Narayin. It works out very well. Dr. Narayin is not quite ready to leave, and you have no place for a cook to work."

I would have liked to pick my own cook, but I suspected that such self-indulgence would turn out to be an exercise in ignorance.

Jagdish had cooked an excellent dinner of fish curry, rice, and vegetables. He stood at the doorway while we ate, occasionally answering questions or bringing something from the kitchen at Mr. Kumar's or Dr. Narayin's request. He seemed a quiet boy, and I would have put his age at about seventeen, but Mr. Kumar told me he was twenty-two, the same age as Judy and I. They assured us that he was honest and responsible. He was a Harijan, or untouchable, and would cook goat, chicken, and fish, but not beef. Since his home was in Barhi, he could live with his family.

Judy made up her mind when she heard that. One of the things worrying her had been how to fit our way of living to the ways of a live-in servant. We hired Jagdish, agreed upon a salary, and placed ourselves for the moment in the hands of Dr. Narayin and Mr. Kumar.

The following morning Judy pumped up our small kerosene stove and concocted a fair imitation of French toast from the local version of yeast bread, which was full of anise seeds. We sat in the sun on the porch of the bungalow, watching the traffic and the goats nibbling the potted plants. When six or seven children came up to the steps, we struggled to talk to them in Hindi. They were Muslims and greeted most of our answers to their questions with wide-eyed wonder. "Such hey?" ("Is it true?"), they asked.

Barhi, in this small dose inside our bungalow gate, was easy to take. If I closed my eyes I could recreate the scene in my head, and since arriving in Delhi this had rarely happened. India was too full of new things, too crowded, too chaotic. Now, sipping tea, laughing with the children, watching quick-stepping peasant women with loads of firewood on their heads move down the road, it was hard to imagine that we had been in India barely a month.

After breakfast an old man shuffled up and touching his hand to his brow in a repeated salute told us that "mukhiaji" wanted to see us. Se we set off on our first visit to a local eminence. We later discovered that B. P. Katriar, the mukhia of Barhi, considered himself with some reason to *be* the local power structure, for he owned the potato cold storage plant which was the only industry in town, he owned the most land, and he had the best contacts with the state government and the Congress Party which dominated it.

B. P. Katriar welcomed us on the veranda of his low, white-washed home and led us into a parlor dominated by family photographs, with overstuffed Western-style furniture and a ceiling fan which hung down through an irregular hole in the canvas ceiling of the room. He had a round bald head with tufts of white hair on the sides and a heavy stomach. He gave the impression through his deep-set, active eyes of a very alert man, sure of his world and his place in it. He sat down on his Western sofa in cross-legged Indian style. I noticed that his white pajamas were of machine-woven cloth, not khadi.

Our protests that we had eaten did not prevent him from summoning breakfast. Great aluminum plates arrived laden with three kinds of bread, potato hash, spinach, a variety of sauces and pickles, and finally several heavy sweets.

From the way he greeted us and insisted that we eat, I knew that B. P. Katriar was accustomed to authority. But his interest in us, in America, was so keen, his awareness so great, that I liked him. It helped that he spoke fluent English, for thus we could even appreciate his sense of humor.

I asked where he had learned so much about America and he told us he had gone to British schools and spent fourteen years as a contractor in Calcutta before coming back to his home in Barhi.

"I think in English, like many of our older generation. My sons do not know as much English—but they have a mother tongue. The British left India railroads and factories, but they were never willing for us to have a language of our own. It kept us weak, so they could rule us. It still keeps us weak."

During the meal he explained to us that Mr. Kumar had told him we would be coming. Mr. Kumar had thought that the mukhia might be able to find housing for us, and indeed there *was* a small house behind the cold storage plant which we might rent.

"Come, let me show you. It's just a few steps back. You will be like members of my family."

We accompanied him to a medium-sized compound set off from the fields by a four-foot brick wall. A low duplex building blocked off half the back of the compound. Half of the building was rented to the manager of the cold storage plant, his wife, and their seven children; the other half would be for Judy and me. The windows and doors were small, but the mukhia assured us he would knock the frames out, poke larger holes in the walls, and put in doors and windows suitable to foreign guests with peculiar ideas about ventilation.

Our half of the house had two tiny rooms, a latrine, and a kitchen, all connected by a brick-paved courtyard. Each room had one electric light, the wires for which hung in a tangle from the ceiling. It was hard to believe that so many wires of so many types all had as their sole objective the sporadic feeding of one naked sixty-watt bulb. Each of the two rooms had a front and back window and a front and back door. Even if the mukhia tore the walls open to put in larger frames, the doors would remain a hazard to anyone over five feet eight.

We discovered that the house was neither concrete like the houses of Dr. Narayin and Mr. Kumar, nor mud like the village huts. A framework of homemade brick bore the weight, overlaid with a smooth plaster made of mud and dung. Newly plastered and whitewashed, the house looked as if it were made of cement. But the walls recorded a history of collisions with chair legs, bamboo poles, and slammed doors, each knock marked by a section of missing plaster.

The roof was formed of semicircular clay drainage tiles laid over a bamboo lattice. Like all such roofs, it would leak whenever a tile slipped or cracked. When the mukhia asked about leaks, one of the workers reported that the kitchen and the bedroom were impossible, though the living room seemed dry enough.

"No leaks? You haven't waited long enough. It is the nature of a tile roof to leak. Mine does."

When we were alone, Judy and I talked over the mukhia's offer. The house was small, but our main worry was the mukhia's comment, "You will be like members of our family." We had heard that villages were often faction-ridden. If Barhi had factions, the mukhia was bound to be in one, and by moving in we might end up taking sides; we might cut ourselves off from half the community. We decided to look around. Both Mr. Kumar and the mukhia assured us that there was nothing else available, but we wanted to start finding things out on our own.

That afternoon we took a long walk around Barhi. The gate of the bungalow opened directly on the Grand Trunk Road, which was the main east-west artery of northern India and ran from the Pakistani border in the west to Calcutta in the east. In the center of Barhi the GT Road, as it was called, one and one-half lanes wide, crossed the Patna-Ranchi Road which had brought us from Rajgir. The town stretched along the cross formed by the two roads. Starting at the bungalow there was an almost continuous line of small shops and buildings. The first building after the cold storage plant was an open-fronted flour mill. A rusty iron sheet supported by bamboo poles sheltered the entrance, and as we passed a haze belched out into the clear air. Inside were ten or twelve old biscuit tins and open wooden boxes containing different types of rice, millet, flour, and maize ground by the clanking mill in the rear. Other boxes held yellow sticks of turmeric, dull red chile peppers, dried molasses, and small split beans: green, pink, yellow, and black. It was more colorful than a Safeway, but I was choking and half-deaf after five minutes of trying to talk to the owner, Karu Sao. He knew of no houses for rent in the village.

The fresh white concrete walls and scrolled balcony of Karu Sao's house next door testified to his prosperity. A dung heap abutted the building, shutting the thorn hedge of Karu Sao's garden off from the road. After that came the village pharmacy, a store selling bolts of cheap cloth, a bicycle repair shop, and several tea stalls serving hot drinks and snacks to truck drivers and other travelers on the GT Road.

At the edge of the pavement were the vegetable and fish sellers, most of them old women with black umbrellas who sat on their heels before wicker baskets full of onions, small prawns, or great carp from the reservoir. A simple scale and a number of rocks which served as weights completed their equipment. Between the vendors on the pavement and the prosperous merchants at their counters were a number of large wooden boxes propped on stilts and shaded by wooden or scrap-iron awnings. These were fruit stalls, betel shops, trinket vendors. Their owners lay on the floor napping, but when a customer approached and cleared his throat they sat up with surprising grace, nodded, and inquired, "What is it today?"

One fruit vendor was more ambitious than the rest. He arranged and rearranged his wares for the best effect, calling out to us, "Fine bananas! Ripe oranges! Sweet, from Assam! Come and *see* my pineapples!" We bought six of his oranges. Peasants came to the tobacco stall next door, laying down a few paise for a single cigarette and a match. That was all that changed hands. Yet the owner would chat with his customer for several minutes while both called out greetings to the passersby.

Even the fanciest buildings seemed unfinished. One elaborate iron fence had been painted with red and green designs, but the painters had left great swatches of paint on the white masonry pillars. Neat concrete stores had been expanded with unfinished wooden props or scrap-iron roofs. Goats wandered among the rice and lentils at Karu Sao's mill.

The fishmongers had established themselves at the crossing, and the crowd of white-garbed men who haggled with them forced the trucks and overloaded taxis careening around the corner to swerve and brake. A banana salesman sat on the traffic island, holding on to a post with one arm and thrusting his heavy brown-and-yellow bunches into the windows of passing trucks with the other. And truck drivers did stop, in the middle of the road, to tear off some fruit.

In addition to the trucks, buses, and taxis, the road carried heavy oxcarts. Globs of grease hung from their axles but failed to still the groan of irregular wooden spokes. Three or four cycle rickshaws passed us loaded with coal and grain. The peasant women with their firewood dodged straight across this stream, followed by scrawny goats.

Judy and I were overwhelmed. We had stopped asking store-keepers about vacant houses; it was all we could do to avoid being run down. When we finally got through the traffic at the crossing, I realized I had been holding my breath. Fifty yards beyond, the line of stores came to an end and a small dirt path led from the bazaar back into the village.

We walked through several separate villages that afternoon, each strung to the others by a line of shops. Narrow paths ran along the sturdy walls of mud houses or the thorn hedges of gardens and cowyards. In the bazaar the men gathered by the radios and fluorescent lights of the tea stalls. Under a shade tree at a turning, a few old men sat on cots and smoked the hooka. Houses? They looked at us in astonishment; ask in the bazaar, they said. There is nothing here suitable for a sahib; we are all milkmen. In another village they were all vegetable farmers. Or Muslims. Each village, it seemed, was inhabited by one or another caste group that met only at the bazaar.

We were relieved to make our way back to the bungalow with its ordered garden, its driveway ending in a neat circle, its doorways hung with blue curtains. The bazaar had exhausted us; the villages seemed to have no room for us. We had plunged bravely into Barhi. Now we knew we needed a retreat.

The warm welcome we had enjoyed at the Katriars' and the simplicity of the physical arrangement were appealing. Living behind them as a "family" might offer us some of the benefits of proximity to an Indian home without an accompanying loss of privacy. And, of course, there was the cold storage plant. Ice cream and ice in the hot season and protection for food in the other seasons were powerful inducements. We were already anticipating the heat. We would have refrigeration without the conspicuous luxury associated with owning a refrigerator in India. (We could not afford one of our own anyway.) The mukhia wanted one hundred rupees a month. It was high, but we had found nothing else. We told him we would move in.

The house, however, was not empty. Surender Prasad, one of the mechanics at the cold storage plant, was living there with his wife and brother. Before we could take possession, the mukhia would have to finish new quarters for them. We were bothered by this "eviction." Did Surender want to move? Why didn't the mukhia build other quarters for us? No, that was not possible. Anyway, Surender was willing to get out, and at the end of our two years he would move back. We contented ourselves with this explanation. Nevertheless, I felt uneasy. Surender's young wife sat on the floor and waved her hand at the smoke pouring from the open fire on the floor, while we pointed here and there and asked for ventilation, new doors, a larger courtyard, a waist-high stove. What were we doing in her house? Did this fit our picture of ourselves as Volunteers—helpful, quiet, unintrusive? Were we living among the people, earning their trust with the new ideas we had brought with us?

We tucked these questions away to be answered later. Surender's wife waved away more smoke and smiled. She said she would be happy to get rid of the smoke, to have a proper stove, to have bigger windows. We were welcome to use the house for two years. The mukhia would be happy to have the rent; we would be happy to have a house of our own; the Prasads would be taken care of in the meantime. Had anyone been hurt?

2.

Once our housing arrangements were settled we could no longer postpone our work. The Peace Corps had led us to see ourselves as catalysts of an educational program in family planning. But the crucial reagents—the doctor in charge and the Extension Educator—were missing. And if they had been present, Judy and I did not yet understand the chemistry involved. Still, it seemed important to give people some sign that we were on the job, even if all we were doing was trying to understand what had happened before we came. The block was large—some areas were over twenty miles from Barhi in a straight line and over thirty by the only available roads. There were more than one hundred villages. I borrowed a map from Mr. Kumar and sat on the veranda of the bungalow studying it. I fixed in my mind the two roads which intersected in Barhi and the reservoir to the north of the block. The map showed no exact features of topography, the strange names meant nothing.

Sitting and studying felt suspiciously like idleness to me, and I was sure it looked that way to everyone else. So I walked to the offices of the block clerk and borrowed the heavy register in which were entered the names and addresses of all two thousand men who had undergone sterilization in the block the previous year. My idea was to do a rough census of areas where there had been progress and areas where work had just begun. I went through the registers searching out the crabbed, faded ink notations of addresses. There were several villages named Tilaiya, and some of the places listed in the register did not appear on the map. But in one afternoon I managed to make approximate notations of the number of those who had been operated on in each village.

Then I filled in the map; one dot stood for five men between fifteen and forty-five years of age in a village. I put a small x for every five sterilization cases. This gave me some idea where people lived and where the receptivity to the operation had been heaviest. More important, it gave me a sense of accomplishment. I had taken a confusing welter of names and lines on a map and turned it into something useful. It appeared that about ten percent of the eligible men in the block had either had vasectomy operations or had wives who wore the intrauterine device. This was a good record for Bihar, but I was hopeful that we could quickly improve it.

I had seen only Barhi itself, and had not yet traveled to any of the other villages. Nevertheless, I spent part of one afternoon trying to figure out why certain areas had proved more receptive than others to family planning. My passion for order was getting out of hand; I finally closed the book and watched the goats.

Judy had been able to plunge more directly into her work. Dr. Narayin had one more week in Barhi, and women had been coming to have the loop inserted. This intrauterine contraceptive is a small, snakelike shape of flexible plastic about two inches long which is placed in the uterus with the end of a thin plastic thread left projecting from the cervix. By feeling for this thread the woman can tell if her loop is still in place; in theory, as long as it is, she will not become pregnant.

Judy assisted Dr. Narayin and the public health nurse, Miss Annama, with the insertions. She returned exhausted and with stories of hot arguments between doctor and patients, of efforts to keep the women in line, of never-ending bookkeeping. Still, seventy women had received the loop. I was excited by the numbers; it was not going to be all that difficult.

The next afternoon I left the goats and strolled over to see how the insertions were going.

The front yard of Dr. Narayin's house had seemed quite large when Judy and I had had tea with Mr. Kumar and the doctor that first day. Now, the mob of village women in tattered white saris overflowed the enclosure and blocked the lane. Some stood in a knot around the front steps; others squatted on their heels with their backs to the steps. As they shifted their weight from

20

heel to heel, their heavy silver anklets clanged, but the sound was almost lost in the cacophony of voices. I first thought a battle had broken out, but they seemed to be conversing normally, like a treeful of starlings at nightfall.

I hesitated to enter, but when I saw the thin figure of Miss Annama, the public health nurse, wringing her hands and looking helplessly at the crowd, I prepared to fight my way through to her. To my amazement a path opened before me. The women did not rise, but without breaking their conversation they waddled out of my way, anklets jingling and saris drawn across faces. At the steps, a tall woman who seemed to dominate the group was yelling at the open door behind which I could see the doctor. The tall woman had shoved two others in front of her and a group of eight or nine milled behind. When she saw me she grabbed the two women and thrust them at me, all the while holding her palms out in a gesture of pleading not matched by her tone. The two women squirmed out of her grasp, my way was clear, and I darted up the steps.

"Oh, Mr. Pope, I'm going to faint, really I am," said Miss Annama. "Look at these women! They've been like this for hours. How can we ever get them in line to do the work!"

"What's the problem?" I shouted.

"There are ninety of them today. The doctor will not insert in those two," she pointed at the two women who had been shoved at me, "because they are not healthy. But they will not go away and we cannot get on to the rest of them."

This was beyond me. I walked back through the crowd, which again parted, and strode over to the block office. I explained the situation to Mr. Kumar who got in his jeep, drove the fifty yards to Dr. Narayin's house, and combining the authority of his voice with that of his horn managed to get the women in some kind of order.

They even stayed in order when the doctor paid them. As an incentive to family planning the government offers six rupees to every woman who has a loop inserted and one rupee to the person who persuaded her to do it. Men who undergo sterilization get twenty-five rupees. All of the women that day were very poor; they had come for the money.

Their number left Judy and me hopeful that family planning was catching on in Barhi. But we both worried about being on our own. If this was the behavior of people in *favor* of family planning, how would we handle a crowd that was against us?

One hundred and sixty loops had been inserted in two days. The villages around Barhi from which the women had come looked good on my map. Judy inspected the dots and crosses. I was envious and wanted my Extension Educator to come so that I too could begin contributing to progress instead of just recording it.

The next day the pharmacist from the dispensary called out to me as I was on my way to the doctor's. He held up a tangled mass of what looked like dirty string. "Look!" he proclaimed with a flourish. "They were behind the dispensary."

"So?"

"You know what they are?"

"No."

He smiled maliciously. "Loops! Thirty-two loops. Inserted yesterday by the Lady Doctor—six rupees for the patient. Pulled out yesterday by the village midwife—one rupee each for her. Plus one rupee she got as the motivator. One hundred and sixty rupees for the women. Sixty-four rupees for the midwife! A very good business, isn't it?"

I held out my hand gingerly. He tossed me the plastic snakes and threads. Little bits of dirt, flesh, and blood adhered to several. I could easily have held five times as many. I could easily have held in my hands the one hundred and sixty loops we had inserted. All I had to do, I knew, was to hunt around the area till I found them all.

How was I to tell Judy? And what did the little dots on my map really mean?

Our new house, with its larger windows and fresh whitewash, was finished. We hoisted our two trunks into a cycle rickshaw, walked alongside it for the two hundred yards between the bungalow and our compound, and unloaded the trunks in our bedroom. We had ordered furniture in Hazaribagh, the district town, but it had not arrived. The mukhia loaned us a string cot and a small stool. We were installed.

We were not so sure we were ready for Jagdish. He was a good cook; several weeks' eating at the doctor's had proved that. But we had been warned to expect some preliminary feints and skirmishes. I was uncertain how to conduct these skirmishes partly because I felt ambivalent about having Jagdish at all. I had a bad conscience. "What the hell are you doing with a cook?" I did not want to identify myself with the people in Barhi who had cooks; they were a ruling class. I had not come to rule.

Buy Judy and I *had* come to work. To work we had to eat. The cleaning and sifting of rice, the slow boiling of lentils, the daily shopping for vegetables and meats, the building of a coal fire made each Bihari meal, however simple, a matter of two or three hours of labor. Most Biharis, of course, had no cook; the wives did this work. For obvious reasons, that could not be our solution, so we found ourselves plunged into a master-servant relationship we distrusted.

Our doubts were compounded by the attitude we found prevalent among Indians. Mr. Kumar and the Katriars, for example, addressed their servants in the familiar form otherwise reserved for children, and they yelled at them. They did no work if there was a servant there to do it. They assured us that reason and good treatment would be interpreted as stupidity, generosity as bad bookkeeping, politeness as fear.

Our consciences prevented our copying this style; we used the polite form of the verb with Jagdish. The value of this gesture was slightly diminished by the fact that we used the polite form with everyone—partly from principle, partly from a fear of misusing the familiar. Judy and I really did not know the familiar forms of the verbs and ended up addressing even each other in the formal manner. Politeness spared us the need to learn a whole new set of verb forms. Jagdish could hardly have guessed which came first, our ignorance or our politeness.

We never yelled at Jagdish. It is not easy to yell in an unfamiliar language; the first effect of anger is incoherence and Jagdish understood no English. We refrained from asking help when we did not need it: we got up to pour our own water; Judy often made tea for the two of us while Jagdish swept the house; she cooked occasional meals. I am not sure how much Jagdish appreciated our resolute independence: I cracked the water jar open on my knee, and I spoiled the broom sweeping out the courtyard.

We got along with less open hostility than we observed around us, but the price was less openness in general. We did not get our way automatically or easily. The first time we sat down to a lunch of rice and lentils we found ourselves chewing a bland white paste with no flavor. Jagdish had not added salt, because, he told Judy, salt would make the rice spoil faster. She assured him that it would not (I am still in some doubt on this point), and that anyway we would not eat rice without salt. Eventually he gave in.

But we were still nervous at having Jagdish underfoot. Everyone told us we must always lock up our possessions, concluding this sermon with the message, "You must realize, this is India." So we were not surprised when Jagdish too began reminding us to lock up the rooms when we left. "Someone might climb over the wall, Sahib." We were touched by this concern but surprised by his persistence. Every morning when he picked up his yellow shopping bag and left for the bazaar he would warn us to lock up and would express his approval of our American combination locks. Finally, when Judy asked him to stop nagging us, he paused in the doorway: "If something is ever missing, Memsahib, you will blame me. People always blame servants. I'm honest, and I don't want anything to happen. You won't believe me."

If Jagdish challenged us to reconcile our position among the privileged elite of Barhi with our ideas and values, the family in the other half of our duplex constantly reminded us how most of Barhi lived. They also reinforced our ideas about family planning. The worst problems of the Prasad family stemmed from Prasad Babu's having had seven children, from the fact that those seven children lived with his wife, his mother, and Prasad Babu himself in the same two small rooms plus courtyard that housed Judy and me, and from the pressure of feeding and clothing those children on the salary he drew for managing B. P. Katriar's cold storage plant.

We first became aware of how precarious life was for the Prasads when dinner was interrupted one day by a knock on the door. I peeked out the window. Prasad Babu's oldest daughter was standing there stretching on her short legs to reach the door latch.

"Yes, what is it?"

She held out her empty hand. "Mashes?"

"You want something?" I asked.

"Mashes. For the fire."

"Oh, one minute." I ducked out of the dining room and pulled a dozen of the unreliable twigs from the kitchen cabinet. She took the matches in her fist and ran back to her house.

That was the first of many such visits. Some nights they needed matches, sometimes when the electricity failed they came for a candle. One week Prasad Babu went on a business trip, leaving the family without money or kerosene for the stove. So every evening we had a pilgrimage of four or five children bringing flour dough, salt, vegetables, and tea pot to our kitchen. Jagdish would set up a chair in front of his waist-high stove and the little girl would climb on it to cook the flat chappatis. Her younger brother knelt on the floor to roll out the dough, and her younger sister carried the hot wafers to their house.

Then Prasad Babu would return and the nocturnal visits would cease, though we always saw the children when we left the house. There were too many of them to remain inside. Their mother kept them going. They were well behaved, worked hard and were usually cheerful. They never abused our friendship. But the coming and going during dinner forced us to confront in our own kitchen the knowledge that what were staples for us were sometimes luxuries in Barhi.

We tried to find other bases for friendship. We had brought along a frisbee and several other toys, but after a day or two they would bring them back and crestfallen tell us, "Ma says we have to work now."

The first month in Barhi was over. Work, or an approach to the work, had eluded us. And while we had touched the edges of a few lives, we had no friends, no sense of what these people were to each other. Now, back to back on our small government calendar were the red dates that marked the Hindu festival of Ram Nomi and the Muslim holiday of Muharram. Perhaps after the first holidays we would understand Barhi better.

Ram Nomi celebrated the birthday of the mythic Hindu hero Rama. It was our first exposure to romantic India. The women wore their best saris. On their heads they carried covered baskets of fruit, incense, and the other offerings to the god. The crowd at the small temple grew thicker. Everyone seemed to be laughing. The women swirled round us in brilliant silks and cottons.

The temple was surrounded by a low platform. We slipped

off our sandals and added them to the pile that littered the base of the steps. Judy was wearing a bright cotton sari, I had on my white khadi pajamas. I thought we blended in fairly well; at least no one was paying any attention to us. We climbed onto the platform and examined the temple. On three sides it had blank concrete walls which supported the tall pyramid-shaped tower; the fourth side had an opening which led to the image of the god. Inside and out the temple had been freshly whitewashed.

I could see no pattern in all the activity. When each woman arrived, she walked several times round the temple. Some were silent, some hummed, some stopped at each corner and bowed, uncovered their offering, bowed again and presented it to the image inside the doorway. A few lit incense, tossed flowers, or cut coconut. Others remained kneeling.

I suddenly realized I was the only man present. I had thought there might be a ceremony we could observe, something we could later ask the Katriars to explain. Instead there was this circling and bowing, bits of prayer, supplications. Each woman seemed to have her own idea of ritual. It seemed random; I was learning nothing.

A loudspeaker hanging over a tree had been blaring out religious songs played on a hand-cranked victrola. The tune shifted, though no one seemed to notice it. Something was familiar, yet somehow wrong. Then I recognized the tune, scratchy but unmistakeable. It was a honky-tonk rendition of "The Tennessee Waltz." The small boy in charge of the victrola was grinning at me. I looked at the women. None showed any sign that the tune might be inappropriate to the prayers and the sprinkling of water on marigold leaves.

I felt a little giddy and very American. Judy and I stepped off the temple platform and back into our sandals. We waved at the boy as we left and he waved back as the familiar piano chords followed us.

Back in the lanes of the village small bands were gathering. In front of their houses the men had hung great red banners, each adorned with the figure of a monkey. Now each banner was carried by its owner to join the others in the quarter, and the groups began to drift up and down the alleys and paths exchanging greetings, bantering about who made the finest show. The procession had no apparent object and no obvious leader. When it had gone on long enough, the banners began to work their way out to the main road and down to the open field which had been prepared for a fair. Women and children tagged along. For several days shopkeepers and tea stall proprietors had staked out their claims on the field. Mud fireplaces had appeared for the preparation of snacks and sweets; thatched walls served as temporary stalls for the display of brass and aluminum pots, glass bangles, cheap shoes and shirts. The merchandise was the same inferior stuff that was sold to the poor in every market; now it shared the glamour and excitement of the festival.

The crowd gaped at the stalls and the banners; we gaped at the crowd. It moved slowly and without jostling. Daily life amidst numbers had taught people to space and pace themselves.

The red flags rested upright against a circle of mango trees, forming a red and green arena around which about half the crowd was gathering. Inside this circle three or four pairs of men had faced off with long bamboo poles. A band of drummers set up a complicated rhythm on long oblong drums decorated with peacock feathers. As the tempo increased, each pair of men started to dance. Instead of using hands and feet to translate the music, they used their staves. I was not sure if I was watching a dance or a mock fight: each move was graceful, each turn came on the beat, but the audience applauded the skill of a parry more than its rhythm.

An onlooker explained that the huge monkey on the red banners was Hanuman, the god who had helped Rama in his fight with the demons, and that the dancers were acting out "stories from our Ramayana." Now I noticed that several teams had discarded their staves and were acting out knife duels, combining gymnastics and wrestling with the dance. Each team followed the same sequence. When one finished, another pair came into the circle. It seemed to be a round, a story built into dance, but within this framework each man had a chance to show his skill. One man in each pair wore a red scarf around his forehead, the scarf always triumphed. The red scarf matched the cherry glow of the banners; the epic of the Ramayana was unfolding, not choreographed for hundreds but arranged for two and repeated hundreds of times.

The onlookers drifted in and out of the audience without, to my eyes, any effort to follow any one cycle through to its conclusion. Like the rest of the fair, the drama was individual, the direction and choreography provided by tradition. The men were not competing. Each concentrated on his own steps, his own moves, his own relationship to the story. Everyone knew that Rama had triumphed, that with Hanuman to aid him he was bound to win. Each of the dancers knew that the ending of the drama had been foreordained. The dueling was steeped in the spirit of the Gita, and of Krishna's exhortation to the warrior: "Concern yourself with deeds, not with the results of deeds."

Muharram, a Muslim feast commemorating the death of the prophet Muhammad's nephew Ali, followed Ram Nomi by a few days. The contrast took me by surprise. I had expected a wake, something akin to Good Friday. Instead the Muslims started the day off with a military parade.

Early in the afternoon the sound of chanting was heard from the large Muslim quarter at the east end of Barhi. From the mukhia's front porch we saw a line of men moving toward us in rank and file, if not in step. Here, on the chaotic GT Road, the organization of these lines was almost frightening. At the front of each group five large green banners were held upright. No group fought for front rank as the Hindus had done. These flags belonged to the nation, and the nation was Islam itself.

Every ten paces the marshals would halt and a wave of chants would roll toward us. "ISLAM, ISLAM, ISLAM: ALI, ALI, ALI: ISLAM, ISLAM!" Then the crescent-and-star banners were raised straight up and the column moved on. Not even the handful of women and children who followed could detract from the sense of order and purpose.

"If I threw one rock now, we'd have a riot," I whispered to Judy. The tension fascinated me. It was real, but at the same time ritual. Barhi prided itself on good Hindu-Muslim relations. Yet every day sparks flew from one incident or another. These individual incidents were too small to ignite the peaceful town. Now, all those tensions were centered in the ranks of marching Muslims. Hindu Barhi stood by, itself divided by caste and family.

B. P. Katriar and Ram Jan Maulwi, the Muslim patriarch, faced this conflict each year. The Maulwi was sitting on the Katriars' porch, and as the procession turned into the compound, the marchers lay their green Islamic banners up against the Hindu walls of the house. The lines broke up, the men jostling each other in an effort to get a good view of the performance to follow. The cadre had become an excited crowd.

A wrestling exhibition began, and in the feints and falls, the grunts and "Oh! Shabash!", tension drained from the crowd. When the lines reformed they were ragged; the chanting never regained its intensity. The fair that followed at the circle of mangoes could have been Ram Nomi. The young men played what seemed to be the same games with the staves, but little of the earlier spirit remained. The mukhia was careful to escort the procession down to the field; the stave fighters hit a little harder, there seemed to be more competition. The Muslims were celebrating a death, not a birth; a defeat, not a victory. And the burden of that death and defeat lay on each one of them. There had been no supernatural monkeys to help Ali, and the Muslims of Barhi counted on none for help today.

3. The week after Muharram our cycles arrived, and we could no longer postpone our first visits to the family planning centers in the outlying villages. The weather had warmed only slightly in the six weeks since our arrival, but the February sunshine greeted us as we set off down the Grand Trunk Road on our bicycles. A slight tail wind pushed us along; the cotton pleats of Judy's new white sari floated behind her. "I feel like an angel, look at my wings!" she called out, tucking her feet up and coasting past me. At the bottom of the hill we passed a pair of bullock carts. The grunts of the oxen and the creak of the uneven axles swallowed up the hum of the wind and the clicking of the cycle gear, so that we seemed to slip by the carts with no effort.

I enjoyed the ride and arrived at the Kariatpur subcenter, seven miles from Barhi, fresh and eager to see how the staff worked in the village. My expectations were tuned to the speed of our bicycles rather than the sluggishness of the bullock carts.

At the Kariatpur Center I met the Family Planning Worker, Priog Mandel. If there had been an Extension Educator at Barhi, he would have supervised Mandel's work, under the general authority of the doctor. But since neither Extension Educator nor doctor was around, I was probably the closest thing to a boss Mandel had. I, after all, was officially assigned at the same level as the Extension Educator. Mandel knew this. He was not comfortable with me. I claimed I had come to help him, yet the first thing I did was to ask him to show me how he worked. Mandel, a tall heavy Brahmin from North Bihar, put a good deal of energy into loud joking. Our uneasiness would have to wear itself out.

Meanwhile, I had to learn everything around me. Before I could judge Mandel's work I had to know far more about the environment in which he lived. So as we wandered down the road, I immersed myself in the sights and smells of Kariatpur, in surfaces that were novel and therefore exciting.

Mandel kept at my side, trying to discern the motives for my coming, motives which he hoped would be familiar and therefore not threatening. While I tried to learn as much as I could, I sensed that Priog Mandel was not at all eager for too many new things. The work, he assured me, was already going "very well."

We walked about a mile to Bersot, the biggest village in the Kariatpur area. Mandel told me that he covered his five-mile working radius on foot. He had no bicycle.

It clouded up, and we reached Bersot in the cold drizzle of a last winter rain. Skirting puddles in the muddy lanes we arrived at the home of the village headman. Mandel introduced me to the headman and the elders who had gathered to gossip the cold away. We sat on the veranda. Several men warmed themselves with clay pots filled with hot ashes, as we had done in Bhui. The headman draped his light shawl over the pot, a grey cotton chimney to draw the heat up to his shoulders.

Things seemed to be going all right. The men knew and liked Mandel; they greeted me warmly. In my halting Hindi I tried to explain who I was, why I had come. We discussed family planning; they agreed on its necessity and assured me their village was one of the leaders—over fifty men in Bersot had undergone vasectomy.

I tried to find out more about their village so I would be able to help Mandel organize his program. Their main concern was the lack of irrigation. They had had a government promise of a pumping set and had dug a well bore. The bore was ready but the government had not supplied the pumping set. "We are very poor, Sahib," the headman told me. "Our land, our hearts, our hands, all are strong. But we have no water. Use your influence with the government, Sahib. Help us get our pump, and you will see how quickly the people listen to your idea of small families."

I told them I had no particular influence; my white skin told them otherwise. I tried to illustrate the connection between large families and the plight of the government: so much had to go for schools and famine relief that there was not enough left for development. But I also told them that I would mention the matter to Mr. Kumar, the Development Officer. This was what I had been trained to do in Lexington: "Always be helpful," the rule book said. Anyway, I was curious about what had happened to the pump set.

When we returned to Barhi, I did speak to Mr. Kumar. He looked from across his desk with its clean blotter and piles of papers at the edges. I wondered how he reached the papers. I asked about the pump. He shrugged. By the time the application had been approved, the money had run out. I had asked him for a larger copy of the map of the block on which I had been entering the numbers of loops inserted and vasectomy operations performed. The map was ready.

He reached forward and rang a bell. A peon pranced into the room, holding up his white dhoti with his hand. I had learned from the Katriars that this style was cultivated to show the world that the man's work could be done with little effort.

"Sir?"

"Get Mr. Pope the map I had made," said Mr. Kumar.

"Certainly, sir!" The peon shuffled the papers on the desk, the ones just beyond Mr. Kumar's grasp, and pulled out a copy of the map. He gave it to Mr. Kumar, who passed it to me.

I was bewildered. Mr. Kumar was healthy, vigorous. He drove the jeep himself instead of using the government-assigned driver. He played badminton at the Katriars'. Yet here he had called a man into his office to hand him a map only two inches from the bell he had rung to call the man! I thanked him for the map. Tea came, we chatted, I left.

The next day Judy and I again cycled to Kariatpur. Judy had spent the previous day observing the trained midwife's work in smallpox vaccination. The villagers shied away from the innoculation because it caused a slight fever. Judy had watched while the team pursued men into the fields, climbed onto roofs, overturned beds. She had to admit that although the enterprise paid off— Barhi was one of the few places in Bihar without smallpox—the circumstances were unfavorable to quiet discussions of the advantages of a small family. Still, she had persuaded the staff that next time they would begin with family planning, in a different part of the village. We arrived in Kariatpur to find everyone equipped for smallpox vaccination. Neither of us knew what to do in the situation.

Mandel had picked a new village to visit. On the way out of Kariatpur he stopped at the school to ask the teacher for the names of the influential men in the village. This was a blow; Mandel should already have known those men well. Ahead of us two collections of red tile roofs peeked over a line of mango trees. The paddy terraces were scarcely as large as scatter rugs; we were walking to the village on the six-inch pathway that separated these terraces.

A series of false turns and retracings soon brought home to me that not only did Mandel not know the leaders of Dulmaha, he did not know how to get there. My hopes for the day collapsed. If he did not know the location of this village, what did Mandel mean when he said that the work was going very well? An old man propped up on the dikes by his stave finally directed us.

The meeting in Dulmaha left me trembling with frustration. We met with a group of Muslims who knew about contraceptive methods, but they had no interest in planning families. Babies were God's responsibility, not man's. No one suggested that God would be angry if they did go ahead and have a vasectomy; indeed, they pointed out that if you needed money badly enough it could be a good thing. Didn't the government give you twenty-five rupees? But until that extremity—well, a man might be able to control the number of his children, but it didn't say anywhere in the Koran that a man *should*, and life was hard enough without shouldering additional responsibilities.

I was able to piece this together from my floundering Hindi, with occasional translations from Mandel. Except for these interjections, however, my co-worker was a sleeping partner, retreating whenever he could behind a newspaper.

When we left, I asked why he had dropped out of the meeting.

"Those were Muslims," he said, "*dead against* family planning." He repeated the English *"dead against."*

"But that's what the government pays you for, to convince people. If everyone was already for it, they wouldn't need either of us!"

"It's hopeless," he said. "All *dead against.*"

After a week of working together, I christened Mandel

"Shakespeare wallah" (the title of a current Hindu film), because each time I saw him he pestered me for a new English book. I couldn't imagine how his rudimentary English could extract much meaning, to say nothing of pleasure, from *King Lear*, for example, but he assured me that the play had been "first class" and that he had liked "the last part best."

When I gave him a new book, we would sit at a tea stall and talk, and Mandel would bluster, joke, and put twice as much of himself into the conversation as everyone else. But faced with villagers gathered together for a family planning discussion, he withdrew. Up went the book, and I was on my own.

Mandel's passion for books and newspapers, for the paraphernalia of the intellectual, was linked with a dislike for the work he did and the people among whom he did it. "People here are so ignorant. In my district, the work would be easy. We could find a few university graduates and explain things to them. Here you can't even find someone who's been to high school. No wonder I can't get anywhere."

He was determined not to try. I had expected co-workers who did not know *how* to work. But I had a set of skills which, although they were not sophisticated, would have made Mandel more effective, and I could have shown them to him fairly easily. I even tried, by example, to do this.

Mandel did not enjoy walking the paddy dikes to Dulmaha, however; he did not want to develop a network of friends in Kariatpur; he did not want to be effective. He wanted to be left alone, to go out once or twice a week and speak to a few men and to spend the rest of his time with his own friends, government workers like himself who felt exiled in Kariatpur. Mandel's dreams could not be realized through any success he might achieve in family planning. He wanted nothing his work could give him beyond the salary and the security. What he wanted was life in an office or a school. I understood his resistance, but my understanding did not help me. Nor could patience help—the virtue most preached in Peace Corps training. Neither would alter the conflict between Mandel's interests and the family planning program. The government needed instruments for the program, but it seemed to have made no effort to select willing instruments. I could not change that.

What Mandel needed was a motive. This motive had to come

from outside his relationship with me. I began to think that it would have to come from above, from his superiors in the Health Department. But neither Dr. Agarwal nor the Extension Educator had arrived. So for the moment I had to regard my work with Mandel as an education in the villages and wait until later to try to change anything.

I felt relieved when Mandel went on a brief vacation, for then I worked with a health worker at Kariatpur, a man everyone called by his last name—Chaudhuri. Chaudhuri's primary responsibility was not family planning, so I had not felt I could work with him while Mandel was around, but he did mix some family-planning education with his assigned duties in preventive medicine and his unofficial but lucrative private practice in curative medicine. That the peasants paid him for consultations showed that he filled a need—I doubted if Mandel even hoped to fill a need. Chaudhuri knew the villages, knew where to find the old men who knew all the gossip. He taught me more in a few days than I had learned in weeks with Mandel. What Mandel seemed to find inexplicable and accidental, Chaudhuri understood and explained, and my picture of the villages as chaotic collections of unpredictable and unreliable individuals was gradually replaced by a picture of the villages as loosely confederated castes and families following rules that were inexact, but no more inexact than anything else around them.

Just before Mandel was due to return, Chaudhuri invited me to his house for tea after work. I accepted gladly. The dark room was divided by bedding which had been hung to air. Chaudhuri beckoned his wife to make tea and to spread a coverlet on the string cot for me. His wife knelt on the dirt floor at the end of the cot and pumped up a kerosene stove. The valve protested at every stroke, but eventually a blue flame erupted. She balanced the crumpled bottom of a teapot over the heat.

Leaning back against the wall, I stretched a bit and felt the tough cord of the bed biting into my bare feet through the cover. The dust which hung between me and the tiny window of light gave the darkness more substance than the mere absence of light. Chaudhuri's wife, circling the stove on her haunches, the veil of her sari always between us, might have been a ghost. The tea in my heavy pottery cup gave off the smell of the hard molasses Chaudhuri used in place of sugar.

I absorbed the eerie room. There was nothing that had to be accomplished. It was a relief from the first weeks of work, from the constant pressure to make each moment serve the purposes that had brought me to India. I slurped tea from my cup as Chaudhuri searched his radio dial for Radio Peking. He and I shared an interest in Chinese propaganda, in the incongruity of old speeches by Chairman Mao. It was a joke between us, but it seemed more likely to bring us together than our efforts to change the poverty of the overcrowded villages.

4. Each day after cycling back from Kariatpur together, Judy and I would sip the tea Jagdish had prepared, talk about the day's work, and speculate on how long it would be before we knew enough to be useful. Our extensive audio-visual training had not yet been needed; no amount of audio-visual aids could improve the presentation of a staff which was not making any presentations. No recordkeeping could increase the efficiency of visits never made. No schedule, however good, could inspire the staff to observe it. All this awaited Dr. Agarwal.

After tea we would wander around the town, visit the Katriars or Mr. Kumar for more tea, then read or write letters and wait for the signal from Jagdish that dinner was ready. He always called us about eight o'clock—early by Indian standards, late by ours. He could not bring himself to put dinner on sooner. During the first weeks we tried asking him to come earlier, but the preparations simply took longer. So we had dinner at eight.

After dinner Jagdish and I would resume the battle of the budget. We had heard often enough that "accounting" was bound to poison relations with a cook, but the first day I sent Jagdish to market I said I wanted a "receipt" for everything he bought. He reported back that evening with a full market bag and a small slip of paper upon which each item and its price had been written in painful English: "meet 2 rupees; kebage 75 paise; rais 1 rupee, 15 paise." I checked the list against the contents of the bag, often asking Jagdish to tell me the Hindi name for the item written on the sheet. Thus I learned that raiz was rice and garet, carrot. The tally added up, Jagdish returned my change. I congratulated myself. Jagdish had made no protest at my request for receipts. Of course, I thought, if Jagdish were not so honest and so unsophisticated, he would probably have found some reason why a receipt could not be had. I had been lucky.

On the fourth day, I glanced over Jagdish's list and discovered that it was in Hindi. "I couldn't find anyone in the bazaar who wrote English, Sahib." I frowned. I could barely read Hindi, and the handwriting on the receipt was terrible. But I painfully transliterated each letter, asking his help, and worked my way about halfway through when I realized what he had said.

"Jagdish, where do these lists come from?"

"I wrote this one. No one spoke English today."

"And the other lists—the English ones. Who wrote them?"

"One of the teachers. I told him what to write."

Suddenly the Barhi bazaar passed before me. The women with their baskets of fish and vegetables, the sleeping fruit vendors, Karu Sao's mill with its open boxes of rice and beans. Where in all of this was Jagdish to obtain a "receipt"? And if he had been able to, what had led me to imagine that the shopkeeper would not write anything Jagdish told him. There were no cash registers, we were rich foreigners, Jagdish had grown up in Barhi.

I sighed. "You don't have to get this list anymore, Jagdish. Every night you can tell me what you bought and we'll add it up together."

We ordered our first chicken. At five rupees for a small, scrawny bird, chicken was the local luxury. But it was also the basis for what Jagdish proudly called his "first-class meal"—a special roast chicken with rice pullao.

The meal was everything he said it would be, and we congratulated him repeatedly. Afterwards I sat down on the bed with the long thin notebook in which accounts were kept, while Jagdish squatted on the floor with his Hindi checklist, occasionally scratching his head to recall items he had forgotten. We went down the list of daily spices—cardamom, turmeric, garlic, cinnamon; then the staples—rice, potatoes, whole wheat flour, lentils, onions; then a few rupees' worth of vegetables and fruit. It was a large bill. Then Jagdish announced that he had paid thirteen rupees for the chicken.

"How much? Chickens cost five rupees . . . at the most six!"

"It's a Muslim feast today, Sahib. The price is very high. You asked for chicken, I bought chicken. That's my duty."

"No, not at that price. Anyone can pay thirteen rupees for everything. You're supposed to get us the right price. Next time something is so high, don't buy it. Tell me instead."

I was angry, sure that the money had gone into his pocket. I thought about taking it out of his salary, to prevent future incidents. But a nagging doubt stopped me. He might have paid thirteen rupees—bad bargaining—but he thought we were rich. Hell, we were rich. Could I deprive him, when he had so little, unless I was sure beyond "all reasonable doubt"? And in Barhi, I was beginning to suspect, I was rarely going to be sure about anything.

I knew these conflicts were rooted in the immense disparity of incomes. Judy's and my combined income was nine hundred rupees a month ($129), about as much as Mr. Kumar, the top government official in Barhi, made. Jagdish earned eighty-five rupees a month. The standard rate in Barhi for a cook was about sixty. A day laborer, if he worked all thirty days of a month, might earn forty-five. Judy and I did not need nine hundred rupees a month; in Barhi we could spend only about six hundred. The rest we saved for trips to Hazaribagh, the District Town, or for leave in other parts of India. We could easily have paid Jagdish more or ignored his padding of the food bill. There was no level of living we could justify beyond the level of living of most of the people around us, and that was a level Judy and I were not willing to attempt.

There would be no more green peas in the market, Jagdish told us one day. "It's March, and the hot season is coming." We bought a second heavy clay jar in which to store boiled water and went to Hazaribagh to place an order for two fans.

The Bihar government had authorized the purchase, promising to reimburse us. We waited two weeks; the days grew hotter, the flies more numerous. We were terrified that the hot season might catch us without our fans, so I went to get them. The dealer reported, with a long face, that he had not been able to find a truck to pick them up at the railway station. "Perhaps tomorrow?"

Tomorrows came and went. Finally the fans arrived, but not

the reimbursement from the Bihar government. I would have to see the Civil Surgeon, who was also chief medical officer for Hazaribagh District and supervisor of the doctors in the blocks, for he had to approve the payment order. Arriving at the district office in Hazaribagh, I pushed aside a blue door curtain, waited for my eyes to adjust to the darkness, and then observed a clerk seated behind a huge stack of ledgers and folders, sticking pins into a pincushion. He rose, greeted me with a namaste, and hastily called a servant to bring me a chair before sending him for tea. We talked about the weather, about America. He asked me who I was, and we discussed Barhi and my work. He inquired about my family. Tea came; it was weak and grey. We drank it while discussing American marriage customs. Several other clerks came in and out, each stopping to congratulate me on my "first-class" Hindi. Finally the man behind the desk asked what he could do for me. I explained and passed him my receipt for the fans.

He looked puzzled by the form and discussed it in low tones with another clerk. Of course, he explained, he was very busy, but since we were such good friends, he would see if he could help me. He opened one of the ledgers and licked his thumb occasionally as he flicked the pages. Finally he stopped, looked very serious, again assured me that he was eager to help and that I would get the money very soon. "But look here," he pointed to a blank section of the ledger, "here is where the order authorizing payment should be. We have not yet received it, though we know it is coming. So we cannot pay you today."

I nodded. I was in no particular hurry. I asked him when it might come. "When it comes, we will pay you." He tapped the desk for emphasis. The heap of wooden pens, wet sponges, ink bottles, and tea cups shook. "But until the order comes . . ."

Jagdish was happy to see the fans but unhappy that I had not been reimbursed. "You shouldn't let the government do that. If money is due, it is due. Suppose they do not repay you?"

I leaned into the breeze from the fan. "I would have bought them anyway, Jagdish. We need them."

It crossed my mind that Jagdish might wonder why we had money enough for two-hundred-rupee fans but felt obliged to complain about thirteen-rupee chickens. I was not sure I understood it myself. It had something to do with my desire to be an insider. India had been scraped by poverty for so many centuries that stinginess was an instinct. I tried to emulate it. Where generosity was a sign of patronizing wealth, I suppressed it. I argued with rickshaw drivers whose spindly legs would have aroused my pity and indignation in America. Hating bargaining, I struggled to master it and searched for bargains that had no monetary meaning to me. Where there was only inefficiency, I suspected duplicity. And yet I was nagged by the feeling that I might not have given the rickshaw driver his due.

If I was not reimbursed I would blame the government, not my own naiveté. Stacks of paper and legions of clerks lay between me and the official responsible. I would never meet him, would never have to worry about how I appeared to him. But I saw Jagdish every day, and I did not want my ignorance revealed to him.

Meanwhile, Dr. Agarwal had returned from Calcutta. The specialists had failed and his son had died. We held back from calling on Dr. Agarwal. So much depended on him, we did not want our first meeting to take place so soon after his tragedy. But B. P. Katriar seemed to think he would expect us to come, if only to call briefly.

Dr. Agarwal was sitting alone on the porch of his house, which was adjacent to the dispensary. He looked very tired, nodded when we introduced ourselves, and apologized for his long absence. We expressed our sympathy and left quietly. I think I was tiptoeing. We felt we should give the doctor several more days to recover before trying to talk about what we had come to do, especially since we were not sure how we were going to do it.

By the end of the week the doctor was back at work in the dispensary. We took that as a signal for a second visit and called at noon, when the crowd at the morning clinic would have dispersed. Dr. Agarwal was at his heavy wooden desk directly beneath a naked light bulb. "Sit down please, Mr. Pope." He was tall, heavily built, with smooth features. His carefully combed hair, tiny mustache, and impassive expression combined to give an impression of extraordinary self-control and reserve. The visible exhaustion was gone. He wore a white shirt and dark trousers, carefully selected though not as flashy as Mr. Kumar's. His hand rested on the stethoscope on the desk.

The dispensary didn't match the doctor's appearance. All the furniture was finished with a dark varnish that soaked up what little light there was. Several ancient anatomical charts on the wall had been stained mustard by the mildew. One corner of the asbestos wallboard covering the ceiling had collapsed, and water stains spread out from its sagging edge. The green upholstered examination table was covered with dust. We began to talk about family planning. Rather, Dr. Agarwal began to talk, describing the situation for us. Although he had done over two thousand sterilizations, practically all were the result of famine—hungry men who needed the twenty-five rupees offered as incentive. Hardly anyone came for family planning advice. Some of this he blamed on the staff. "Frankly, they have no real idea what the work means or how to do it. Do you agree?"

We shifted nervously in our chairs, suspecting that we could tell him nothing new. Cautiously I described my difficulties in working with Mandel. He nodded: "We can make no progress until we do something about the Muslims."

I knew that the Jana Sangh, the Hindu religious party, opposed family planning, claiming the Muslims would not practice it and would outpopulate the Hindus. Had Dr. Agarwal these rumors in mind?

"It's not a claim; it's a fact. They won't. Last year Mandel brought in ten men, all Muslims. When they got to the steps here, one of the mullahs met them, told them family planning was against the Koran, and that was that. They all left. It becomes harder with time. People remember how Muslim majorities led to the partition in 1947. They fear more partitions. Anyway, they are afraid of both the vasectomy and the loop. But in a month or so things will pick up, when the peasants are again short of cash."

We had hoped for bolder marching orders. We asked what he would like us to do. He asked our opinion. Where was the work most needed? Citing figures on my map, I mentioned several areas where little progress had been made. He shook his head. No staff was near enough. Finally he looked up. "Why don't you continue working with Mr. Mandel, Mr. Pope. Mrs. Pope, I think you should work in Barhi. It's not safe for you on the roads. The truck drivers can be nasty." It was the end of our interview.

Judy was mad. "I came to do a job—the truck drivers just leer anyway. Looking at my short hair, they're probably not sure I'm a woman."

We were in a dilemma. Should we follow instructions or try
to get around them? Should we give up all the hopes we had pin-
ned on Dr. Agarwal's arrival? Were we being fair? His son had just
died; he had been away a month, knew nothing of us and little of
our ideas. We decided to wait to see what Dr. Agarwal would do.
We arranged to go with him on an inspection trip to Kariatpur.
Surely Dr. Agarwal would be better able than we to interpret the
real attitudes of the peasants toward the family planning program
and its staff.

At two o'clock one afternoon we heard a horn at the front
gate. Girja, the driver of the medical jeep, informed us we would
be leaving in about an hour. When we arrived at the dispensary,
we found Miss Annama and one of the midwives from Barhi who
worked with her, the pharmacist from the dispensary, and
Husseini, Dr. Agarwal's attendant. Would the jeep be taking us
all? Girja was watching from the porch, a broad grin on his face.
Dr. Agarwal appeared and nodded in my direction. "Don't
worry, Pope Sahib. We'll fit them all in." Had he been reading
my mind? Eight people in a small jeep. Well, I thought to myself,
it's only seven miles.

Dr. Agarwal took the wheel and Girja sat in back. The doctor
said that he liked driving, he did not feel the need of being
driven. Judy and I sat in front with him, ostensibly so we could
talk, but I suspected that our status as Americans was being honored.

Dr. Agarwal described his experiences as a military surgeon
on the Kashmir front, his first job. He compared the army with
the Bihar government, to the discredit of the latter. Discipline
was good in the army, paper work minimal, procedures efficient.
He had been stationed far from his wife, but he preferred military life. His posting in Barhi was a disaster. Barhi was small, the
practice limited, offering almost no chance to pursue his real
love—surgery. He said he wouldn't mind if all government doctors had to spend some time in small villages. But with the system today! "If you know a few people you get your first posting
in a big hospital and never see a village. If you offend one of the
top officers you can spend twenty years moldering in the block
dispensary. Soon I'll be playing the game, stacking up the names
of my friends and relatives until I have a big enough pile to get

away to Patna."

Dr. Agarwal did not expect the situation to change. He didn't like his job, Barhi, or the government. He said nothing of the needs of the hundred or so patients he examined each morning at the clinic. Because he had led the state the previous year in vasectomies, I had expected some enthusiasm for family planning. Instead there was resignation.

When we pulled up at the Kariatpur subcenter, I caught a glimpse of Mandel, tucking his white shirt into his dhoti and skipping along in his sandals in an attempt to reach the center before the mighty doctor sahib.

Chaudhuri, Mandel, and Miss Sylvia, the nurse-midwife, greeted the doctor, who sat at the table and asked to examine the staff registers. Miss Sylvia was first. Timidly she edged forward, the end of her sari clutched in her teeth, her eyes averted from the terrible sight of her supervisor. She perched the registers on the edge of the desk, daring to go no closer. Dr. Agarwal pulled the books toward him just as they were about to fall off. Miss Sylvia backed away against a pillar. Calmly, precisely, Dr. Agarwal examined each section of the register, circling in red ink each mistake and irregularity, stopping frequently to dip his pen, pausing at the end of each page to let the ink marks dry, and commenting in a factual tone: "Time of last menstruation should be entered at the time of the first antenatal visit to the pregnant women."

His meaning flew somewhere over the terrified girl's head.

Mandel came next, shuffling his registers like a deck of oversized cards and checking to see that he had them all.

"Are they all here, Mr. Mandel?" the doctor asked.

"Yes, sir."

"Let's look at your contraceptive distribution list."

Mandel shuffled again. And again. "I can't find it, sir."

Mandel's registers were in worse shape than Miss Sylvia's. Mandel was not timid. He spoke up after every comment to defend himself and to assert that the doctor's way "just wouldn't work." Given the military tone of the whole procedure, I was surprised that Dr. Agarwal did not object to this impertinence. I could only conclude that the doctor's pessimism about discipline in the Bihar State Health Services embraced his subordinates as well as his superiors.

Only Chaudhuri was ready, and as the doctor turned page after page, asking questions to which Chaudhuri gave quiet answers, the health worker's smile broadened until, like the Cheshire cat's, it seemed independent of his face.

But watching the doctor inspect Chaudhuri's work, I was puzzled. There were no questions about field technique or the response in the villages. Most of the data in the registers had little relevance to what had to be done. Dr. Agarwal approached the inspection as an accountant. He seemed most concerned that the columns be consistent. When he had finished with the columns of figures, he was finished.

The British administration, designed to collect taxes, had hung on like the English titles and forms; here were the new administrators, recruited from agricultural workers, doctors, and teachers whom the New India had sent to the villages. But Dr. Agarwal did not approach his own profession as if he were a tax collector; in the dispensary he was energetic in servicing his patients. I wondered if he would bring that same dedication to his work with the other medical staff members. What Judy and I could do might depend on the answer to that question.

Our relations with Dr. Agarwal remained formal. But when we explained that we felt inspections with all their paperwork were not the ideal way to train the staff for family planning, he agreed. He decided, therefore, to call a monthly meeting of the staff. We were elated. We would no longer have to wander through the labyrinth of the registers. We could begin, with Dr. Agarwal, to grapple with the question no one had answered: how to make family planning take hold in a stagnant rural economy like Bihar's. Our brief encounters in the villages had given us a few hints. We knew that the staff was not prepared to convince individual families they should limit the number of their children. Mandel's tentative visits and even more tentative presence on those visits gave no peasant any reason to trust him. Miss Sylvia was too shy to explain her own ideas, much less to change someone else's. The rest of the staff was similarly disadvantaged.

Judy and I told each other that family planning failed to take hold largely because no one understood it. When old men said, "children are the gift of God," they were not arguing theology; they were stating truth as they knew it. We had to shake the faith of the people in that truth. Nor was that the whole task: even if they knew they could control their fertility, many of them would not choose to do so. The idea of planning was foreign. Riding along the road one day, I was stopped by an old man who asked why Judy and I were always going somewhere. I told him we worked in family planning, *parivar niogen*, and asked if he knew about it. "Yes, certainly," he replied, which meant, "I am being polite by agreeing with you." I pressed him. Yes, he understood the word *parivar*: mother, father, sister, brother. Everyone knew what a family was. But "planning." Surely that word *niogen* was an *English* word?

Although the concept of planning did not seem to exist in the dialect of the old men of Barhi, I hoped that we could train the staff to explain contraception, one way or another. We wanted them to show people condoms and loops, to draw simple diagrams of sterilization, to make regular visits and begin building trust.

So we prepared our campaign. We bought six or seven colored bottles of ink from the druggist Nagu Sao and made ten sets of simple diagrams for the staff to use in the villages. For the moment we forgot to ask, "Why should Mandel want to do basic education on the condom?" We would have dabbles of ink and cardboard so that he could. Perhaps having the pictures would make the work more interesting, less threatening. The important thing was that we had something we could do, something we could finish, something that was ours. After four months in Barhi, we needed to say "*we* did that."

About an hour before the first monthly meeting was to start, we gathered up the diagrams, a box of condoms, a bag of loops, and tied them down on the rack of the bicycle. Jagdish came out on the porch.

"Where are you going, Sahib?"

"To a meeting at the dispensary."

"What's this, Sahib?" he asked, picking up a foil-wrapped condom labeled "For prevention of disease only. . . . Made in Akron, Ohio."

"That's a condom, Jagdish."

"Condom," he enunciated, smiling. "For family planning. Show me how to use it some time. It must be a first-class medicine."

"Where are you going?" a high voice asked behind me. I turned. The youngest of the children next door was standing there, smiling.

"Here, catch," Jagdish called out, throwing him the condom.

"What is it?" the boy asked, looking at the bright foil.

"Condom," Jagdish told him. "It's for stopping babies. Show it to your brothers and sisters."

I thought of the label: "For prevention of disease only." I thought about the American battles over sex education. Perhaps it would be easier to explain contraceptives in Barhi.

The meeting had been scheduled for two o'clock. We arrived on time to find an empty dispensary. Panditji, the wardroom attendant, came along to open up. We asked where everyone was. He said it was not yet time. We told him it was after two.

"The meeting is at two o'clock, but two o'clock Indian time," he explained.

We sat down to wait. Eventually the staff showed up, laden with their registers, and finally Dr. Agarwal joined us, empty-handed. Earlier we had discussed with him our ideas for the meeting. He had his own ideas. He placed great emphasis on correcting the registers and said that he intended to give each of the staff a target for the month. Each man would be required to prepare twenty patients for vasectomy, and each woman would have to prepare twenty women for the loops. This was the only way the block as a whole could meet the target which had been set by the District Office in Hazaribagh. Judy and I were uneasy about targets. They were unrealistic, as Dr. Agarwal recognized. More important, they did not fit in at all with our idea of slow education, and since Dr. Agarwal admitted that the staff would not be penalized if they failed to meet the targets and would not be rewarded if they succeeded, the targets were meaningless.

Judy pointed out that if the nurses did prepare twenty women a month for the loop, Barhi had no Lady Doctor to insert them. "Really that's better," Dr. Agarwal said." The village women are not suited for the loop anyway; it has too many complications. It will be better if we can't insert them. But we must give the nurses targets anyway. If we don't, they won't know what is expected and won't work. If we prepare the case and cannot do the insertion for lack of a Lady Doctor, we can always indicate in our quarterly report, 'so many cases prepared but not inserted

47

due to absence of assigned Lady Doctor.' So there's no problem there."

Judy tapped her fingers impatiently on the bench but Dr. Agarwal's calm military mien gave no hint that he saw anything humorous in the statement. I let it pass but wondered how the patent insincerity of these goals would affect Mandel. Thus far he had at least been waiting for me at the subcenter; would I now have to fetch him from his house? I could not understand Dr. Agarwal. This man had worked day and night during the drought. He had personally visited the scene of every cholera case, on foot or by bicycle if necessary, to see that sanitation was maintained.

The staff sat silently while Judy and I explained our diagrams and showed how to demonstrate the condom. They agreed that our ideas were "first class," "very fine," and tucked the condoms, the loops, and the flash cards under their seats. Dr. Agarwal gravely followed our presentation by issuing an order that the staff carry supplies. "Enter that in the record," he told the medical clerk. The order was duly logged and read back to the doctor.

Then the doctor inspected and criticized everyone's registers. In exasperation he finally wrote the proper forms in English on the blackboard. The meeting went on and on. Judy and I had long since lost track of the number of orders given to the staff, most of whom were as confused as we were. Dr. Agarwal's supervision was thorough, his instructions exact, his words carefully chosen. No general could have given clearer orders, but no general would have given half so many. And no one had trained the privates to understand the orders.

After the meeting I asked the clerk what would be done with the minutes he had kept. "Oh, they stay here in the file."

"Then what are they for?"

"If we didn't write the orders down, then we wouldn't have a record. And next month when the staff comes in and hasn't followed them, we wouldn't be able to prove we gave them."

I suggested to Dr. Agarwal that he might distribute the minutes. That way the staff would at least have a record of all the columns and forms he had given them, so that if they were interested they could correct things.

He shook his head. "That won't do. It is *their* responsibility to write down what we tell them, to ask questions. If we start writing everything down, they will simply stop listening at the meetings. It would be most unsuitable."

"OK," I said. "We'll see how many of them keep track of these directions."

He sighed. "Yes, we'll see. I don't have much hope."

Neither did I.

Dr. Agarwal had pointed out to the Civil Surgeon, his superior in Hazaribagh, that while some women wanted the loop, there was no Lady Doctor. I knew that he didn't want a Lady Doctor, and he knew it, but the Civil Surgeon did not know it. To be more exact, Dr. Gope, the Civil Surgeon in question, did not care. However, Dr. Gope had several Lady Doctors who were supposed to insert loops, assigned to the hospital in Hazaribagh. But in Hazaribagh there were not enough patients. So Dr. Gope announced that a Lady Doctor would come to Barhi once a week to insert loops, and Dr. Agarwal told the trained midwives in the subcenters that now they could really begin to meet their targets, and the midwives went out to the village houses and told the women that if they came to the subcenter at eleven on Friday the doctor memsahib would come to insert the loop and the government would give them six rupees.

That Friday the midwives brought some village women to the subcenter—not at eleven but at ten. It was a slcak time of day for the women—they had no watches. They waited until twelve, the time for preparing the midday meal, and then left. When the Lady Doctor arrived in the jeep about two, she was tired and angry that there were no patients. Only Judy's firm insistence that the women had been there saved Miss Sylvia from a scolding. Miss Sylvia trembled anyway, but it was our one advantage as outsiders that no one questioned our honesty. No one could understand our motives, so everyone assumed they were disinterested. Hunger and disease, or the fear of them, were the mainsprings of life in Barhi. They did not touch Judy and me.

The Lady Doctor agreed to come early the following week and to send the jeep to pick up the women. We waited at the subcenter, but the jeep returned empty. The doctor wanted to know what had gone wrong this time. Miss Sylvia bit the end of her sari. The driver of the jeep spoke up. "The women won't come. Today is a feast day, and they say it is unclean to have the loop inserted today."

I turned to Chaudhuri, who had been watching. "Is today a holiday?"

He laughed. "Who knows? Every day is a holiday for someone. This is India."

I nodded. I nodded again when Miss Sylvia whispered that the women had known the doctor was coming, had not mentioned the feast, and had said today that they had not known last week that the feast was coming. No one ever knew when a feast was coming. No one ever knew a week in advance when a government holiday was coming, though they were marked in red on every calendar. People made appointments and then simply failed to come.

When the third week arrived, the women came but there was no jeep and no doctor. I had had enough. Thus far I had tried to prod someone else into action. That day I got on my cycle and pedaled to the electric power substation, which had a special telephone circuit I could use to call Hazaribagh without waiting for the trunk line on the public system, which was usually out of order.

"Hazaribagh 225, please," I began. "Hello, Sadar Hospital. Is the Civil Surgeon Sahib in? This is Mr. Pope calling from Barhi."

Static.

"Hello, is the Civil Surgeon there? This is Barhi calling!"

"The Sahib has gone to the operating room." I had to guess this response, I couldn't actually hear it. The peon who answered the phone in Hazaribagh held the receiver away from his mouth so he wouldn't contaminate it.

Eventually one of the clerks took the receiver, angry at all the noise. "Yes, what do you want? What is all this shouting?"

"This is Mr. Pope in Barhi. Can you please tell me if the Lady Doctor is coming to Barhi today?"

"How would I know? Ask the Sahib!"

"Is the Sahib in?"

"No. He's gone to lunch."

"Could you find out if the jeep went to Barhi?"

The jeep was valuable equipment. The clerks kept much better track of where it went than they did of the people who went with it.

"Oh, the jeep. One minute, please." The clerk came back and informed me that the jeep had not left; it had not left because the Civil Surgeon had been busy that morning and had not had time to give the doctor the keys or the money to buy petrol.

So the women waited in the sun, Miss Sylvia chewed her sari, and everyone's opinion of everyone else's unreliability was confirmed. Judy and I, too, began to say: "Nothing can be done because no one can be trusted."

5 . The Bihar government soon put an end to our strata-
gems by aborting family planning. Painstaking consultation of
textbooks had convinced someone in the Ministry of Health
that they should order a complete survey of every couple in
the state. Dr. Agarwal and I calculated that it would take three
years to complete the survey. In Barhi, which had a full staff,
it would take four months.

I was relieved that we would be excused from accomplishing
anything. It was a mammoth Mickey Mouse exercise; even
Mandel might be able to take a census. And then it would be
done. Since I didn't care how the census came out, I could quit
pushing the system so hard. This was a job the system was up to.
So Judy and I began pushing the staff into a round of village
visits: day after day, neighborhood after neighborhood, we asked
the same seven questions. Most houses stood empty, so we relied
for our data on the old women, the chatterboxes of each quarter,
and ended up listening to much gossip.

Everyone promptly lost all interest in family planning.
Should we have fought harder? But how? If Judy and I were to
boycott the census, we would simply be letting Mandel,
Chaudhuri, Miss Sylvia, and the others carry the load. So we
went from house to house and tried to see that the staff entered
the numbers in the proper columns.

More to prove our reliability to the staff than from any sense
that it mattered, we tried to keep them going. Long columns of
names, ages, numbers of children built up the registers. The government theory that these lists would be used to plan visits to

each family with children flew against the fact that it would take years to complete the task. Barhi Block, according to the census, had 63,000 inhabitants. This meant that there were about six thousand couples in the childbearing group. The total family planning staff for the block was two male family planning workers and one Block Extension Educator, who was not there, to visit the six thousand men; and one public health nurse and four nurse-midwives to visit the six thousand women. As the lists grew longer, I grew numb. We would arrive in a village quarter, briefly exchange the news, and begin filling out the forms. At first I tried to build up a mental picture of the families as we listed them, but numbers overwhelmed me. And in April and May the heat got worse. We worked on the census in the early morning and late afternoon.

This madness reached its peak at the end of May. With the thermometer over 115° and the hot sandy wind sucking the water out of our bodies, Mandel and I would depart at six in the morning for a scrub forest, where we would seek out and census small villages of Santhal tribals with sixty or seventy people in each. Mandel hated the work, and I couldn't blame him. But I did blame him for complaining.

I carried one-half gallon of water, frozen solid in the cold storage plant. This not only kept the water cool; it rationed it as it melted, so I could not drink it all in the first half-hour. Mandel carried none and would not drink mine because I was not a Brahmin. Worse for him, the tribal villages had no concern for caste at all. So when Mandel was supposed to be searching out the one track in the scrub forest that led to Singrama, his thirst was driving him to find a school and its teacher. Teachers were almost all Brahmins, so each school became an oasis in a wilderness of wells and water jugs from which Mandel could not drink. But in his forages for water we often lost the road to the village.

The Santhals were a tough hill people with a reputation for friendliness and honesty. Their villages were small and open. In the large Hindu villages all one saw in any direction were narrow dirt lanes, children whose bellies were swollen with worms, and piles of manure. Here the lanes ended in a bamboo thicket or corn patch, and eyes and mind could escape the poverty. There was no way to escape the heat, however, so after ten days I accepted Mandel's claim that he had censused the remaining villages without me. The fakery no longer bothered me; I knew Mandel would never walk that far just to give a family planning talk anyway. Or so I told myself. I was no longer asking Mandel to give anything to his work. Was it the beginning of realism, or fatigue?

Shortly after we had "completed" the census, I was standing in the courtyard one evening with a glass of iced tea from the cold storage plant. Jagdish came out of the kitchen and knelt beside his grinding stone to roll out the spices for dinner.

"Sahib, that Mandel came by this morning."

"Oh," I remarked cautiously. "What did he want?"

"He wanted to see you. He said he had to come in anyway to pick up his paycheck."

I laughed. "Mandel comes in to pick up his monthly paycheck about five times a month. As soon as he has picked up one, he begins looking for the next."

"He was complaining about the sun, about how you made him walk and walk and walk in the sun, though he was dying. I told him, 'Oh, yes, Sahib is very hard worker.' He had nearly collapsed of thirst. 'Jagdish,' he said, 'I was five hours in that sun without a single drink of water. My head still hurts.' "

"So I said, 'Sahib had water. Did you ask him for some?' "

" 'Oh no, Jagdish,' he told me. 'I'm a Brahmin. How could I drink the Sahib's water?' "

"Sahib," Jagdish went on, addressing his question to the grinding stone, hesitating before he continued, "I have a deep question." He paused, as if waiting for permission to ask it.

I put down the glass of tea.

"*Why* do people say what Mandel said . . . that they can't drink water from other people who are not Brahmins? Why?"

I don't remember my reply, something feeble and not very helpful or perceptive. It was unimportant compared to Jagdish's having asked the question.

Jagdish knew the rules of caste. He knew what it meant not to be a Brahmin; as a Harijan it meant, in most eyes, to be nothing at all. He had never known anything else. But he did not know why he lived by the rules. He expected that I could explain why Mandel felt superior to him. He must have seen that I did not respect Mandel but did respect him, a Harijan cook. He had seen that I had some standard different from the one he shared with everyone else in Barhi. He wanted me to explain this different standard.

I was caught. I felt superior to Mandel in no small part because I would eat Jagdish's food and Mandel would not. Twenty years ago my indifference to caste would have seemed irrational to everyone in Barhi. Now, caste was beginning to lose its hold in the kitchen, though the barriers to more intimate mixing remained firm. I could describe this change, but Mandel could not. He could not see it because even the slow pace of change in Barhi had passed him. That gave me, in my mind, an advantage. It meant that I, and not Mandel, stood on the side of change in Barhi. But how cheap this superiority was! None of my emotions were bound up in caste; I was not part of it nor it of me. The part of me that grew angry had no idea why Mandel refused the water. I failed completely to comprehend the meaning of caste for Mandel. Worse, I had not offered him the water. I *knew,* or thought I did, that he would refuse it. In the same way Mandel would have *known* that it was dirty to drink water at the house of a Harijan. I had never asked Mandel to explain what he felt. Therefore I never guessed that neither Mandel nor Jagdish understood why they lived by the rules of caste. I had answered that question in my mind with the common Bihari saying, "It's just that."

Jagdish's life was shaped by caste. He needed to understand "why?" He needed to know that there might be something else. I had answered him with a shrug which permitted me to keep my sense of superiority over Priog Mandel.

As the hot season advanced, Judy and I put less of ourselves into our work. We had less energy, and anyway the elaborate organizational chart that purported to show flows of authority and communication within the Bihar family planning program represented little more than protocol: people at lower levels stood up and waited for people at higher levels to sit down. There was nothing more in the way of supervision, training, or leadership. Channels of communication could be blocked on either side. Dr. Agarwal, I was convinced, wanted direction from Hazaribagh. But Dr. Gope, the Civil Surgeon, could not give it. Dr. Agarwal wanted the staff to share his personal dedication—but Mandel and the others could not feel it.

The heat made everything seem less important. It hung heavily in the house; only in the evening did a cooling breeze stir, though it did not penetrate our screens. We would wander outside, drinking cups of tea, or walking along the dry riverbed where small piles of charcoal and white ash marked the sites of recent funeral pyres. The bones waited for the monsoon to sweep them down to the sea.

Usually we ended up at the Katriars', and as we sat and talked or listened we would think about our relationship with our landlord, with the mukhia. What kind of man was B. P. Katriar?

After dinner he would relax in front of his house, a circle of chairs around him, waiting for Barhi to call. Any friend who came to enjoy the tea or the cool breeze or the conversation shared this privilege—for on these evenings B. P. Katriar held court for the people. Friends could serve as counselors, but B. P. Katriar was king. The official government courts handled most of the legal cases, the violations of government ordinance. But the mukhia was still the final appeal for the peasants and shop-keepers who were involved in petty disputes on which the government would not rule. Barhi had no social workers, no ministers, no juvenile court. Tradition, the rules of caste and religion, and the authority of the head of the family provided guidelines for resolving conflict. Perhaps these guidelines had once been sufficient, and the castes and communities autonomous and self governing, but change had broken in on Barhi and someone was needed to mediate between old ways and new. Who better than B. P. Katria, whose family house had stood in Barhi for over one hundred years, yet who himself thought in English, had spent years with the British in Calcutta, and who by building the cold storage plant had himself wrought change?

So the mukhia thought. His personality dominated the proceedings. Anyone could come and present a problem, but then he must wait patiently while B. P. Katriar set the tone. If the request was pronounced reasonable and just, the thing was done. A means would be found, if not by the mukhia then by someone else present, to grant the request, to find a path through the bureaucracy to free the loan or to control the peasant's father-in-law.

If the man was "absurd," his request unreasonable, everyone joined in the measured ridicule—measured, because no one was to

56

be driven away for good. The man who came this week asking to be relieved of his taxes might be foolish, but the mukhia preferred him to return the next week with a proper request, a request the mukhia could grant. Otherwise the network of obligations would fray and important decisions might begin to escape the mukhia's grasp.

The best breeze blew through the mukhia's front yard; his daughters served the best tea, and B. P. Katriar was the best conversationalist in town. But my real reason for joining these sessions as an observor was to expose myself to aspects of Barhi which otherwise remained invisible. People came to the mukhia only when the resources of their own family and caste had failed them. And these problems were often hidden not only from Judy and me but from the government.

The arrival of a government official in a village signaled the end of conflict. Once he sat down in the chair which every village mukhia keeps for officials, once he had pronounced, his decision was accepted as true and wise. Only when the official got up from the chair and was escorted by his host out of the village did the host quietly explain to him the true state of affairs: the villagers were unwilling to pay back the loan, they did not trust the Muslims to keep their side of the bargain, the women feared the smallpox vaccine. None of this information existed officially, and in any inquiry the headman had the whole village to witness that he had told the official no such thing. In this way officialdom could know what was going on without anyone's taking the risk of telling the truth. The official in turn passed his information up the hierarchy the same way. His ledgers and reports glowingly detailed advance on all fronts and gratefully acknowledged the wise direction from the ministry. In private, over tea in the office, the doctor would explain to the Civil Surgeon that his requests were impossible, his staff insufficient, and local cooperation nil.

This entire system assumed official dishonesty. The village headman quietly relayed the truth to his superior. But Judy and I were not dependent on the system. Therefore, since people believed we were honest, they never trusted us with the truth.

The mukhia's audiences were altogether different. People brought their disputes to him for settlement. It was not the government pursuing them for information, it was they who pursued the mukhia for help. So the audiences took place "on the record." The private remark had to be trustworthy; on it alone could the mukhia decide. If the Development Officer found out after a meeting that the peasants had lied, he would shrug; if the mukhia discovered that someone had lied to him in these audiences, he would be furious.

This was one of the few government institutions in Barhi to which people came by choice. Yet I winced at the full force of the mukhia's authority. And though I never saw him deviate from his own ideas of fairness out of prejudice or personal interest, I knew that the entire proceeding was designed to insure that petty conflicts did not become magnified to the point where they challenged the personal prestige of B. P. Katriar.

Half fascinated, half horrified, I watched and listened. Not all those who came had a clear idea of what they wanted. One old man complained that the wells were drying up, as they did each year. The mukhia arched his eyebrows and threw up his hands. "What am I to do?"

The old man repeated his story. People had to haul water from long distances; the mukhia must tell them what to do.

"Do? Haul it!" the mukhia exploded. Pointing back at the cold storage plant, he snapped at the man, "You think your wells are the only ones that go dry? My own is down twenty feet. I have thirty thousand kilos of seed potatoes stored, and each day I must check to see if there is enough water to run the plant."

I was surprised at his anger. As the old man continued to whine, the mukhia turned away and noisily slurped his tea. The old man hobbled off into the darkness. I decided that the key comment had been "My own is down twenty feet . . ." Wealthy businessman that he was, the mukhia was worried. The old man had made him think about an unpleasant subject, had reminded him that he was emperor only as long as he was rich, and that one season of real water shortage could wipe him out.

On another evening a man came with the complaint that his landlord owed him money on a loan. The mukhia seemed skeptical; the man was an outsider from North Bihar. He sent a servant to call the landlord. The servant returned without the landlord but said that the man's wife had sent their nine-year-old son instead. As soon as he saw the tenant who had complained, the boy began to sniff and said that the man "hit my father." The mukhia sat back, as if his suspicions were confirmed.

He looked at the tenant who was standing stiff with his hands clasped behind his back. "Well?"

"Yes, sir. I hit him. He wouldn't pay back the loan I gave him."

The mukhia tapped his fingers. "How much?"

"One hundred rupees."

"On what terms?"

"He was to pay me thirty rupees a month for two years."

The mukhia's arithmetic was faster than mine. "You say you came here to work," he roared. "I say you came to rob! That is three hundred and fifty percent interest a year! I ought to have you locked up in the police station. Do they allow such robbery where you come from?"

The tenant stood more stiffly than before. "Sir, that is the agreement we made. He said he would pay me, and he owes me."

"He owes you money! Scoundrel! Is that why you hit him?"

"Yes. He refused to pay."

Suddenly the mukhia sat back very quietly. "So you are not only a usurer, but a policeman, judge, and magistrate as well? In your district each man is his own law? Perhaps things have changed since I was there last."

"I did not take the law in my own hands, sir. I came to you tonight."

At this point the servant who had brought the boy spoke up. "Sir, the woman says that he has not paid the rent since he came."

The mukhia smiled. "Is that true? How much rent do you pay?"

"Twenty rupees, sir. Why should I pay, sir, when he owes me more than that each month?"

The mukhia turned to the rest of us. "Have you ever seen such a thief? He comes and plays money lender when he cannot even pay his own rent. He is a big man, he can hit people, but he doesn't cover his bills." He turned back to the man. "You have not paid the rent in four months, since you came?" The man nodded miserably. "That is eighty rupees. You loaned him one hundred, which leaves twenty. There is no question of interest here. You will give him twenty rupees for having struck him. And I don't want to hear anything more from you. If you have to make trouble, do it at home." The mukhia turned away, and the conversation shifted to the price of grain.

Our own living situation sprang to mind. B. P. Katriar did not want us as commercial tenants, though he charged us a high rent. We couldn't be "friends"; the age difference was too great. We couldn't be clients; we needed too little. He wanted us as family; then our prestige as Westerners would add to his. I talked freely to his daughters; Judy was invited to his kitchen to learn how to make Indian breads and pickles. He opened the figurative door-ways of his house to us, but this still left open the question, "How closely related are we?" Judy and I had to decide how far into the family we wanted to go. There was no shortage of op-tions. The extended family offers a pattern for almost any kind of relationship, and the universal forms of address, even to strangers, are family terms: mother, father, son, grandfather, cousin, father-in-law.

From the beginning we had been welcomed at the Katriars' for breakfast: potato curry, flat chappatis, mango pickle, and three or four sweets. We tried to limit the quantities of food lad-led onto our plates. We would say no three or four times, but each refusal provoked another summons to the servant to add more to our plate. Then we would politely place our palms over the plate. The food was ladled onto the edges. Then we tried to use both hands as umbrellas and found the next spoonful of po-tato curry landing on our wrists, while everyone laughed.

Finally we learned to eat slowly and leave a little of each dish on the plate. This slowed the torrent.

We were still mastering the art of eating with our fingers. The mukhia ate more than we did but spent less than half the time at it. His hands were quicker than our eyes; they had to be. Other-wise he could never have accommodated both his voracious ap-petites—for food and for talk.

His paunch testified to his skill at the one, and we discovered that he was almost as good at the other. He spiced his anecdotes and observations with witty arrogance. "We Brahmins are sup-posed to be the mind of Hindu society; we are supposed to teach, without worrying about how we will eat. Now we eat without worrying about teaching." "Politics has become a school for scoundrels. The old guard had something. Look at Nehru. Now the jackals have driven the honest men out. We can do nothing. I am a Congressman, and I have always been a Congressman. Last election I wanted the nomination from Barhi; they gave it to an outsider." Here he tapped his bunched fingers against his forehead two or three times and shrugged. What could he say about such folly? Really, the man was amazing. He continued, "The local delegation came to see me. They wanted me to run as an independent. They implored me. 'Save us, save this area. You know that the Raja has ruined us.' "

He laughed. "The Raja's son, who holds this seat, is an idiot, never finished eighth grade. And they knew that I was really out for the people, not myself. So I asked them, 'Will you work, will you deliver the votes?' They all said, 'Oh, yes, just give us a chance. Our people are fed up.' So I ran."

He paused to down some more curry, then picked up a round milk sweet and squeezed the syrup out of it until the spongy milk solids squeaked. "The Raja's son ate me alive. I was winning two days before the election. Then the Raja and the Rani went campaigning." He shrugged. "You know the village of Ichak, south of here? Well I had gone there at the request of the Muslim leaders to a private meeting. We met at the house of the village mullah and I explained what I could do for their area." He gestured with his saucer to indicate his surroundings. "At the end, they agreed to support me. They meant it. I had no hold over them." He laughed. "But then the Raja heard. He has friends in every village. He sent the Rani." His grin widened. "She drove into the village, stopped the car in front of the first Muslim house and got out. Then she went into the kitchen." His eyes rolled. "What an event! 'Rani miri ghur me chelyai.' ('The Rani has come into my house.') Within two minutes every woman in the village was there. She gave a simple speech.

" 'You all know,' she said, while the women giggled at the idea that she had entered a village house, 'what I have is yours. I have one son—he is yours. Now he has said to me, "Mother, if I do not win this election, I will never marry." It is in your hands whether my line, which is your line, lives or dies. If my son loses, our line dies.' And she picked up the hem of her sari, stepped into the car, and drove off. Five minutes it took her."

"And the result?" I prompted him.

"The women went to their husbands—who knows what they said or did—and the Raja carried every vote in Ichak. That happened everywhere. But it served me right for abandoning the Congress at my age. I am too old to change my color. Not like some of these young chaps."

His capacity to mock himself seemed rooted in his complete Indianness. He could laugh at caste, while Dr. Agarwal seemed embarrassed by it. His grandfather had dominated Barhi from this house; he could do so as well. He had learned the language of the West, mastered its engineering skills, used its economics. But he had not tried to assimilate its spirit. Dr. Agarwal, Mr. Kumar, the other government officials in Barhi—outsiders all—called him "Katriar Sahib," employing the title they themselves inherited from the British. But Barhi called him "Basadeo Babu." *Sahib* means master; *babu,* father. The doctor sahib's power was from outside; he was an intruder. B. P. Katriar was part of Barhi and shared its history.

The Katriar family pleased us, as they were bright and lively. We didn't worry about making mistakes, knowing they would forgive our ignorance and guide us through the profusion of daily choices. We wanted their guidance, but we hesitated, a little fearful of the dominant personality of B. P. Katriar.

The mukhia did not cow his wife as he did the villagers. He was by far the strongest character in Barhi, but his wife was by far the strongest woman. She ran her household with the same meticulous attention that her husband devoted to the business, and neither interfered with the other. Both could rule from a chair; both sensed the moment when personal inspection would help. Judy and I would stumble across each of them in what, for Barhi, were very unusual circumstances for a boss. Ignoring his paunch, the mukhia would scramble up a ladder to make sure the new tiles had been laid correctly on the roof, pulling a row off in anger and hurling them to the ground when he found mistakes. Mrs. Katriar would move through the storeroom swinging her keys and suddenly kneel down to examine a sack of rice. When the mukhia was absent, his wife stood watch at the cold storage plant. She would summon one of the laborers to place her chair where she could oversee everything. Elsewhere in Barhi men did not take orders from women.

Four of the mukhia's children were at home. Morari, twenty-six, was the eldest, and his wife had joined the household. Morari had vague political ambitions but was without his father's verve.

Arun, twenty-four, and earning his M.A. in Economics, was friendly and bright—drifting, gathering opinions from others, always absorbing but not saying what he thought. Shobha, nineteen, had been to college but played the role of the docile youngest daughter. Her mother when young had traveled by rail all over the state to visit friends and relatives; Shobha never stirred from the nest. Anuj, seventeen, was a likeable high school student who seemed to be waiting for something to happen.

Judy and I puzzled over how such a distinctive couple could have produced such bland children. They did not seem dull or thwarted, but the formation of personality had been delayed. Exposed to the tough wills of their parents, prevented by tradition from opposing them, the four younger Katriars had little chance to develop individuality. Underneath, character was forming, but it did not surface.

Only Morari's wife asserted herself, for as the eldest daughter-in-law, she was expected to prepare herself to take over a household which would one day be hers. She had a sharper manner with the servants than the others, less time for banter and joking. Like Mrs. Katriar she carried household keys tied to her sari, and on occasion she swung them with authority.

She had paid a price. She revealed to Judy that the two of them were the same age. Judy gasped. This mature woman with two children and the responsibility, in Mrs. Katriar's absence, for a hugh household!

"How can that be?" Judy asked.

"I was married at fifteen," Morari's wife replied.

So we remained distant relatives of the Katriars. We were unwilling to submerge ourselves in their household, just as Judy was unwilling to abandon her own identity for that of an Indian woman. The family would compliment Judy on her saris and bangles and press her to grow her hair long like an Indian woman and give up her silver earrings for gold. And each time Judy answered, "But I'm not an Indian. I'm an American!"

It was proving hard for Barhi, even after five months, to take us as we were. It was proving hard for us to define our own position. We worked in the Health Department but evaded its rules and regulations; we lived in the Katriars' compound but rejected the mukhia's authority. We had to; we needed independence if we were to change anything. But the people with whom we dealt had so little freedom that our own cut us off from close friendships.

By the end of May the heat had obliterated such concerns, and indeed all curiosity. As the dry heat intensified, everything shriveled up. The river vanished and the water in the wells receded. By midday the buildings in Barhi seemed to have retreated from the heat that beat down from the sky and radiated up from the earth. The awnings on the fruit stalls and tobacco stands came down, shutters and doors slid shut, the baskets of vegetables and fish were gone. Even the Grand Trunk Road was abandoned, its shimmering asphalt surface quite empty.

At first, in April, we had simply cut out our midday activities and slept like everyone else. Two fans kept us dry, a tall mango provided some shade over the courtyard, and Jagdish abandoned the kitchen while food cooked, piling pots and kettles on precarious scaffoldings of broken bricks. About five in the afternoon we got up, drank water or tea with ice and praised the chance that had located us behind the cold storage plant.

Tomatoes were gone from the market, leaving only six or seven tasteless varieties of gourd and okra, which Jagdish learned to fry in oil so that they lost their slipperiness. I began to lose weight. At lunch I could barely make myself toy with the never-changing menu of rice, lentils, and fried okra; rice, lentils, and fried pumpkin; rice, lentils, and fried gourd. Dinner, with the first cool air sucked through the window by the fan, was easier. The water hauled from the well with more and more labor by Jagdish became heavier and heavier with salts and minerals and after boiling was opaque. A still breeze blew in the afternoon, carrying dust and sand from the riverbeds and fields. The rounded red tiles of our roof seemed to catch each grain and dropped a stream of grit on our bed, the table, and closet. Judy and Jagdish could not keep the place clean with the stubby village broom. I was too tired to care, but as I lay on the bed Judy would rage about slamming doors and shaking her fist at the roof while a gentle rain or dirt fell on my glasses.

In late May the quality of the heat changed. The fans brought no relief at night, they simply blew great guests of hot air. Our bodies couldn't pump sweat fast enough. I clattered out to the well with buckets and rope, and having hauled the water for the next day, would return one last time dressed only in shorts. I would hurl the bucket down the well mouth, wait for the gurgle as it filled, and then lift it quickly and pour it over myself. The relief lasted five or ten minutes until my hair and shorts dried, but the memory of the freshness helped me sleep underneath the fans.

Judy finally found the answer. Offices hung great reed mats soaked with water over doors and windows so that the breeze would cool as it passed over them. We tried the same thing with sheets, but too little moisture evaporated. Then Judy discovered that if she wet her clothes, with their folds of cotton, and lay down beneath the fan, she would actually be chilled. Sometimes we didn't use the fan but would fall asleep with wet clothes, sleeping until they dried. Then, gasping, we would run to the bathing room, pour a bucket or two of water over our heads, swallow a glass of iced tea, and return to bed. Eventually we were eating, cooking, sleeping, and reading in wet clothes.

There would have been nothing to look forward to in the entire day if it had not been for the cold storage plant. Judy and I learned how to make freezer ice cream in the plant, and soon the daily bowl of ice cream had become the ritual around which everything else revolved. Every morning I beat up a quart of milk, added chocolate or orange flavoring which had been sent by our parents, and carried the aluminum pot to the plant. Here in great vats of supercooled brine sat the heavy molds for the ice. At one end was an open channel, where I suspended our pot from a string. By noon it would be frozen.

I would get up then, wrap a lungi (a sort of sarong) around my waist, and emerge into the glare of the sun. When I got into the plant it took a few minutes for my eyes to adjust to the dark. Then I would reach down, unhook the pot, and carry our ice cream back. The aluminum pot transmitted its cold to my hands as I walked back to the house, feeling the sum swirling through my head, walking carefully, fearful that I might trip. I carried that ice cream like an offering to the gods.

Sometimes the laborers, in the process of unloading ice, knocked over our pot. There was no greater catastrophe. I would hold the heavy pot of salty water and milk, tears pressing against my lids, wondering what I had done to deserve this, barely able to make myself step into the sun. And as I walked back each crack in the earth would burn itself into my brain, and I would curse the heat.

Usually Judy and I sat around the table, spooning out the ice cream for the three of us while Jagdish watched. He ate his bowl in the courtyard, while Judy and I went into the bedroom and lay down. Savoring the chill, we hardly noticed the taste; and when we had finished, we lay bloated, pitying our friends in other towns who had no ice cream.

By evening the pleasure had worn off and we would anxiously listen to the evening news for word of the progress of the great monsoon rains, across the Bay of Bengal, over Calcutta, toward the Chota Nagpur Plateau and Barhi. A few clouds would creep up in the afternoon, as though building courage to approach the sun, but they always retreated as it set. The wind grew stronger, the dirt worse, the well-water sank lower. One day in the first week in June, while lizards scrambled across the roof over our heads, I realized that the wind had stopped. Then the other noises outside—leaves, cow bells, and distant traffic, faded away. Only the fan clacked on. I got up, opened the shutters and peered into the courtyard. Everything seemed blanketed with a yellow dust. A yellow layer covered the sky. Above, the wind was still blowing, but on the ground everything was still. Then the back row of trees in a mango grove vanished in the yellow . . . and the sky grew darker. Hastily I slammed the shutter.

"It's a dust storm," I told Judy, excited at this bit of the desert come into my house. "Everything's dark and yellow."

She got up and looked. "I can't see anything. Are you sure?"

The fine dust began seeping through the cracks and holes in the roof. The darkness lasted only a few minutes, and when the light returned . . . everything was covered with a thin dusting of yellow. But real clouds had taken the place of a blue sky. It seemed cooler, and suddenly a great rush of fresh air swept through the mango grove. We ran into the courtyard, hoping, but only a few drops of rain fell. The breeze, though, had come from the rains. It felt clean, washed, and almost as welcome as rain. The children next door were outside playing, and Judy and I sat down on the well rim and tried to taste the wind.

We wandered over to the mukhia's. He was sitting outside and greeted us with a smile. "It's coming! I told you it would. In a few days the monsoon will arrive." Judy and I laughed, delighted. Barhi wasn't so bad at all. We had made it! No one could say of us "only mad dogs and Englishmen go out in the noon-day sun." We felt for the first time like old hands; we had mastered the art of survival in Barhi. Things were going to look up, I was sure of it.

We had been invited to Dr. Agarwal's for tea. We knocked on his door and heard a radio playing inside the bedroom. Dr. Agarwal appeared, dressed not in his usual pants and shirt but in a lungi and a long shirt called a kurtah.

"Good afternoon, Mr. and Mrs. Pope," he said quietly, holding aside the door curtain. "Come in. My wife and Dipak are in the bedroom. Please join us there for tea."

The bedroom was dark. Mrs. Agarwal and Dipak, their three-year-old son, were lying on the bed. The doctor turned off the huge radio set on the table; then stepping outside the room, he quietly asked his servant to bring tea. When he saw that we were still standing, he asked us to sit down.

We slipped off our sandals and sat on the bed. Judy chatted with Mrs. Agarwal about the baby while the doctor and I waited for the tea. I noted that Dr. Agarwal had hung one of the garish calendars of the gods found both in poor village homes and in traditional wealthy houses like the Katriars'. Otherwise the furnishings were "Western," that is, modeled after those the British had used, an awkward compromise between Indian materials and colonial taste. Though high-ceilinged and painted a cool green, the room lacked the ease of the Katriars' far less pukka parlor and seemed to have lost something in the compromise.

"Carl," Judy said, "Mrs. Agarwal wants to know about family life in America. I've told her about weddings and love marriages, and I mentioned that you call your mother and father by their first names. She doesn't believe me."

"That's right," I said, shifting into Hindi since Mrs. Agarwal understood little English. "I started doing it when I was little and they got used to it."

"I think," Dr. Agarwal broke in, changing into English, "this casual upbringing is the cause of all the drug problems and hippies you have in America. Almost all college students take drugs there, and there is very poor discipline in the universities."

"That's really not true, Dr. Agarwal. There are some drugs around, but I would say that discipline in American universities is no worse than here in India." It irritated me that he had shifted to English. If his wife wasn't interested, which was possible, American manners dictated that we should talk about something else. Judy changed back to Hindi, but we became quickly frustrated. Dr. Agarwal had read more about America than most Indians and refused to listen to any information that clashed with his interpretations. At the end of five minutes he was telling us what our culture was like. We introduced gentler topics.

Dipak had been reaching for the doctor's stethoscope on the bedside table. Judy had noticed him playing with it in the dispensary, so she asked Mrs. Agarwal, "Is Dipak going to be a doctor when he grows up?"

Mrs. Agarwal giggled, "Who knows? Ask his father."

Dr. Agarwal sighed. "I hope not. Really I don't know what he can become. Not a doctor or an engineer, I pray. Of course, it's his decision. I can't tell him what his interests are." He changed into English again. "Things are getting worse, not better, in this country. The population is growing so rapidly that by the time Dipak is grown, doctors and engineers will be down the drain. Really, unless we do something quickly, I have no hope."

The servant came in with tea. I caught a whiff of cinnamon, and something sharper.

"Is this spice tea?" I asked the doctor.

"Yes, and it's very good. You put cinnamons and cardamoms in the boiling water. Also, we use the best Darjeeling leaves. It's expensive but worth it if you really like tea. You can get it in Hazaribagh. Try it."

I carefully balanced the large white cup on my knee and waited while the doctor passed a cup to Mrs. Agarwal. Dipak immediately reached out. "No, Dipak, not this time," the doctor gently chided.

Mrs. Agarwal laughed. "He always wants tea. It's not good for him, I know, but sometimes we give him a little."

The tea was everything the doctor had said it was. "This is the best tea we've had in India," I told the doctor.

He smiled. "I don't think you know much about tea in America, Mr. Pope."

"You're right," Judy said, and I was relieved to find some note on which we could agree.

6.   At noon the day after our tea with the Agarwals, an electrical storm knocked the power out. The monsoon had come. When the high wind and lightning stopped the rain began to fall straight down, first gently, then steadily, then increasing to a downpour. It continued for half an hour. The next day it rained harder; and then for three days the rain kept us inside. Judy and I began talking to each other again. We lay on the bed in the afternoon writing letters, listening to the radio, or reading. Sometimes I just lay back and felt my arms against my face. So cool. I felt like a snake that had just shed its skin. I wondered if I had any sweat glands left. Would I grow a new set before the next hot season?

The rain on the roof was familiar; it was the same sound that rain made on the roof at home. Jagdish was whistling and his food tasted good again.

After dinner, when the rain had stopped, we walked. Roadsides were carpeted with new grass and small plants. The water buffalo moved almost lightly, toward the pond. The river was running, and the sisum trees had shed their old leaves.

Another cloudburst, at dusk. Children ran through the bazaar in the gullies of rushing water, splashing the crowds of gossips who stood under the awnings of the shops.

Day after day the rain fell, sometimes only a quick evening shower, sometimes a whole day of thundering water. Early in the morning we woke to the thudding of the oxen moving out to trample and plow the paddy fields, and at dark I could hear men at the well, washing the thick mud off their legs.

Everyone around us was busy, and after a week of simple pleasure it was time to look around and take stock of ourselves. Six months had passed, long enough to explore many blind alleys, long enough to learn what wouldn't work. We would have to start fresh, but we knew more. We knew how isolated we were.

I should have understood Dr. Agarwal —he was the most westernized member of the town's small elite—yet I did not. His stiffness and formality never yielded. Neither Judy nor I knew why he called those weary monthly meetings, or why he crippled them by refusing to circulate minutes or provide the staff with material they could understand. We did not even know if these two attitudes were in conflict or if they had some common source.

We could see that he was torn between modern and traditional India, between pajamas and trousers. We guessed that we intensified this conflict. Would we accept his credentials to modernity? To prove himself to us, he seemed to close himself off from traditional India, from Barhi Block itself, from his own staff.

We did not threaten the mukhia; anything he borrowed from us was a gracious concession. That was his strength; he used Western ideas without losing himself. As he showed in his audiences for the peasants, he could translate those ideas into traditional terms.

Judy and I knew that we could not really explain Western ideas in Barhi, but we wanted to help Mandel and Miss Sylvia do so. Here the mukhia was unwilling to help; he wanted to keep his unique position as interpreter.

Neither Dr. Agarwal nor the mukhia saw Judy and me as we saw ourselves, as potential helpers. We entertained the mukhia, we threatened the doctor, we bewildered the rest of Barhi. But in the rebirth of the monsoon I regained my confidence that I would find someone who shared my hopes, who needed my skills and attitudes to supplement his own.

I went looking for new friends, turning to the khadi shop. "Khadi" had a double meaning. It symbolized my ability to use traditional Indian culture in a comfortable way; it was the mirror image of the mukhia's strength. And the closest historical parallel to what I wanted to see happen in Barhi was the Ghandian movement, which had taken khadi for its symbol (though I was unsure that the government's policy of subsidizing it was economically sensible). Khadi was simply a way of saying that Barhi and I could find common ground in other than the colonial tradition. I never explained this to anyone. It was enough that when I wore khadi on the bus, I would hear an occasional comment, "Sahib must work with Vinobaji." (Vinoba Bhave is the leader of what remains of the Ghandian movement.)

The khadi shop in the bazaar was next to the biggest tea stall. Two great slatted wooden doors bore a small white-and-black metal sign which declared that the Barhi Block Sarvodaya Khadi Bhavan was open 10 to 6. The sign could only be read when the shop was closed and the door shut, which was most of the time. The store's "Manager Sahib" lived in a whitewashed room above the shop and came down when the rattling of the doors announced a customer. On market days, however, the shop stood open, and the young government servants of the town whose homes were in other districts and who had no roots in any of the villages gathered there. I joined them.

The young men came because they were bored and wanted to talk. My presence added to the interest, for I was an ambassador of the rich, mechanical, materialistic United States. No one recognized my self-assumed role of village worker in khadi.

One of the young men, Guruji, was employed by the agricultural department as a plant protection expert, doling out DDT and more dangerous pesticides to illiterate farmers. He was fighting off his parents' attempt to marry him and claimed he wanted me to find him an American bride. But he pleaded busy whenever I told him that an unattached American woman would be visiting us! The Inspector of Schools, a Muslim, called on me to referee his debates with the Hindus over the relative virtues of Urdu and Hindi. Since Muslims always told me that I spoke their dialect, Urdu, while the Hindus claimed that I was talking their Hindi, I was considered impartial. Of course, I was unable to make a decision, and this repeated confession puzzled everyone. Surely I, who spoke both dialects, could tell the difference? Alas, I could not. I mixed them up shamelessly, like most people who spoke the village dialect, Hindustani.

There were more or less regular visitors to the khadi shop, but they usually left it up to Manager Sahib to explain India to me. He did, at great length, with a broad grin, employing a sanscritized, highly elegant Hindi that I couldn't begin to follow; then he would nod in the direction of the Schools Inspector and cast his comments into a deeply poetical and mystical Urdu that totally eluded me. Then he would stop, chew his betel nut, and wait for me to confess that I had understood nothing.

"But Pope Sahib," he would say, "I meant . . ." and he would tell me in Hindustani, all the while looking at me with an expression that said "you have a long way to go."

I enjoyed these games and always felt welcome at the shop. But we never got beyond games. Somehow the little circle always broke into two groups—Pope Sahib and everyone else. I was an honored guest, but we were all constrained by the need to behave as guest and host. I seemed imprisoned in the role of Pope Sahib. I never knew if the Indian genius for labeling reflected the impossibility of dealing with such vast numbers of people as individuals, or if the fact of multitude and the sense that people were dust, grew out of the labels. But the label that stuck to me was "Sahib."

I argued with Manager Sahib. "Please don't call me Pope Sahib," I would say, "Those days are gone, colonialism is dead. Aren't we friends?"

"Of course, Pope Sahib," he assured me.

"Then use my name—Carl."

"Kal?"

I laughed. "All right, call me Pope bhai ('Pope brother')."

He grinned. "Pope *bhai*." He leaned out over the doorsill to spit out his betel. "Oh, Guruji" he called out, "come here and meet my new brother."

Guruji walked over, neatly sidestepping the red betel stain. "Namaste, Pope Sahib," he began.

"No, no," Manager Sahib interrupted him, "not Pope Sahib. This is Pope *bhai*. He says the days of sahibs are gone." They both laughed. Then they tried to explain to me that sahib didn't really mean "master" anymore. It was simply a polite form of address. In a sense he was right. I did, after all, call him "Manager Sahib." And on the bus there was "Driver Sahib" and "Conductor Sahib." But these were job titles, whereas I, like the British master before me, was simply referred to as "Sahib." The title was always there, wherever I went. It stuck to my white skin like beggars at bus stops, waiting for me to acknowledge its presence, to answer to it, to confirm my privileged status.

I continued to be Pope bhai in the khadi shop, but the barriers between us lowered only slightly.

When I carried my luggage on my head like a porter because I didn't want or need a porter, because carrying luggage on my head was easier, and because I wanted to make a point, people who bumped into me on the railway platform smiled and used me as an example. "There's a sahib who does things for himself. Our own sahibs should do the same thing." But I was still a sahib. And the porter could not play his role, which was to carry my luggage. I was not a porter, yet I was carrying luggage. He had to persist in his efforts to take my bag, or give me some other title such as "suspicious sahib," "You don't trust me Sahib?" "Really Sahib, I am most reliable coolie. I have fourteen years in this station."

But if I accepted the role of sahib, I accepted the gulf between Barhi and me. A sahib is settled firmly on his side of the line, the peasant on his, and to communicate they will both go through B. P. Katriar. As a sahib, my hope that someone would need me, that I could help change Barhi, would evaporate.

It was going to be hard enough to find a real job anyway. Judy wondered if people had any idea that we had been on earth before coming to Barhi, or that we would go on living after we left. No notion of the distances, geographic or social, which separated Barhi from America could take shape within the small circle of the villages. When we went on vacation to Calcutta, Delhi, or even to Hazaribagh, old women would ask Judy when we got off the bus, "Have you been to see your mother and father?" Our repeated explanations, "No, it's too far to America, it takes thirty hours by airplane," meant nothing to the village elder who explained to his grandson that America was very far away, in the direction of Delhi, "as far away as the home of Indira ji, the Prime Minister."

As Peace Corps volunteers, we had identified ourselves from the start with the family planning program, and that meant with the government. We told people that our cycles and rent came from the Bihar government. Ladies who came up to me in the bazaar, perhaps to plead for an illegal abortion or to ask a question about Judy's hair, would hail me with the salute brought to

India by the Moghuls, the gesture of respect for authority. They addressed me as "Oh, Sarkar!" ("Oh, Governor!")

Mr. Kumar, the doctor, the block staff in their stuffy cement bungalows, the Police Inspector with his jeep and teams of red-turbaned constables were all "sarkar," all outsiders. None lived in the village. Their three-year postings were designed with exactly that in mind. The government feared that if its staff put down roots in the villages, instead of residing briefly in towns, corruption would become unmanageable. The transfers did not prevent corruption, but they made it evenhanded. If they took bribes, the local leaders (like village headmen) could adjust the sums to the means, the caste, or the family of the man asking the favor. Votes, support in a village feud, prestige could substitute for money. The transfer system prevented too much favoritism; it created a purely monetary market for corruption. There were two kinds of graft: honest and crooked. An honest clerk, as the family planning workers all solemnly assured me, was one who took twenty rupees to get you a transfer and got you the transfer. A dishonest one took twenty rupees and did nothing. They lamented the decline in morality since independence; there were very few "honest" clerks left.

The transfer policy also insured that services never reflected local needs or conditions, that officials operated at one-third or one-fourth of their capacities. Mr. Kumar, who expected a transfer within a year, still didn't know the names of all the village leaders in the block. Clerks, who often evaded their own transfers, came to hold the real power through their greater knowledge. The Hindi term for the result is the contemptuous phrase, *Kiranni Raj*, the "Rule of the Clerks."

If this was the consequence of a policy of three-year transfers within the Bihar Civil Service, what did it imply about the Peace Corps idea of a two-year term of service by young Americans? We were isolated Westerners in an isolated town of government servants, themselves untrusted, unneeded, and largely unknown by the surrounding villages.

And Judy—Judy found herself a memsahib. A sahib may not carry his own luggage, must pay higher prices, and will always find the porter at the station hauling his luggage into first class even if he shows a third-class ticket. Otherwise he is expected to work, to be useful, to have skills. A memsahib is permitted none of this; Indira Ghandi notwithstanding, status, women, and work do not easily mix in India. The traditions of Hindu patriarchy, Muslim purdah, and Victorian stuffiness insure that most men never deal with any woman as friend or equal.

They recognized that Judy was different, so they did not mind sitting next to her at a wedding. But in her work she was confined to the female sphere, which in Barhi meant the house. It was awkward for social theory that Judy had to go from house to house to do her work, just as it was awkward that the public health nurse had this responsibility. Insofar as they could, men on the road pretended that Judy did not exist, though this did not prevent them from staring, openly and directly. They never greeted her with the casual "Namaste, Sahib" that I was accorded.

When Judy stepped back from this limbo into the proper woman's place in the home, she found that even her limited view of the village world was broader than anything other women saw. Women in Barhi managed their households with virtually no interference from their husbands. If the family was large or wealthy, the wife might have a great deal of power. But it was power within the circle of family relationships. Most village women lacked the vocabulary, not to mention the experience, to discuss politics, history, or geography.

Of course, there was always something to talk about: there were two ways of boiling rice, washing babies, and catching husbands—Judy's way and theirs. Her way was a source of endless amazement to the village women. If the two methods turned out to be the same, this was just as amazing, for they had no fund of experience from which to predict or expect—all Judy's answers to their questions were equally startling.

If there were two ways of doing something, the conservatism of village life dictated that theirs was right and Judy's wrong. Rice with salt was not rice at all. It didn't take long to determine that things were different in America, so conversation tended to break down into criticism of Judy. Her fear of seeming arrogant prevented her from extending the argument, at least until she returned to the bedroom and could express her feelings to me.

We had to guard against assuming that only we were isolated. After all, Judy's position as a woman was no different in principle from that of the nurses with whom she worked. They too, assigned away from their families as a matter of policy, were without relatives in a society that defined the limits of a woman's world by the farthest relative she could get to see. Mandel complained about the gap between the villager and himself. Mr. Kumar knew that he could never learn the truth of any incident without the help of B. P. Katriar or someone else who belonged. Dr. Agarwal felt that his surgical skills were rusting. And much, if not most, of what Judy and I felt seemed part of the price paid for trying to graft modern techniques onto villages which had no words for them. But we felt the isolation more keenly, precisely because overcoming it would not threaten us. Our checks would arrive every month from the Peace Corps in Delhi. A fine, air-conditioned hospital in Calcutta waited if we ever needed it. Our plane tickets home would be issued when our two years were up. We could afford to worry full time about how to work in Barhi village because we were never going to have to live off it.

Miss Annama, Judy's first co-worker, had been replaced by a new public health nurse, Mrs. Srivastava. Mrs. Srivastava had come because of a mistake, triggered as it happened by the efforts of Peace Corps staff to insure that each Volunteer had at least one co-worker. For a while Judy had two, but pay was available for only one. Eventually Miss Annama left. The treasurer in Hazaribagh refused to issue Mrs. Srivastava her back pay, unless she gave him a large slice of it. This was honest graft, but Mrs. Srivastava was a stubborn woman and balked at paying. Judy and I felt responsible, so again I donned my sahib robes and went to Hazaribagh.

The treasurer agreed that the technicality under which the money had been held could be waived and I returned with Mrs. Srivastava's money. Dr. Agarwal's comment on the episode was that "No one else could have done it, Mr. Pope. The Treasury is quite incorrigible."

I could do that, but I could not devise a strategy for successfully carrying out the assignment that had brought us to Barhi. Nor could the staff. They had other, more personal and immediate interests. They were devising strategies to insure there would be food in their stomachs.

The rains continued throughout June and July. Most days began with a sky of grey dotted with blue; in late afternoon it would turn black and purple, and a white cloudburst would lash down while I took shelter in the nearest house or tea stall. We couldn't get to the villages by bike because of the mud, and anyway the pace of work in the rice fields kept the villagers out in the paddy all day. We did manage to cycle to the subcenters and explained to the staff how we would all work together when the planting was finished. The staff enjoyed these conversations since for the moment we asked nothing of them: the rains were a legitimate excuse for doing nothing. Our visits did little for family planning; the Barhi State Health Department as an institution could not do much to help, and so far I had not persuaded any of the staff to initiate anything.

Then in late June the state employees demanded a cost-of-living wage increase which had already been granted to employees of the central government. The state government refused, pointing to an empty treasury and blaming the central government for policies which had caused the inflation in the first place.

The union of state employees called a strike. At least, someone called a strike in the name of the employees' union. There was no strike vote; no one on the hospital staff knew that a strike was coming until the newspapers announced it.

Judy and I were at the hospital when the news broke. Mrs. Srivastava had just finished thanking me for the fifth time for obtaining her pay from Hazaribagh. When the clerk came in and announced the strike her eyes gleamed. She liked the idea of compelling the government to give increasses, yet she realized that I wouldn't be able to protect her in this fight. She turned to Judy. "What does this mean? Will they fire us all?" She gathered her sari around her.

Judy laughed. "Who would replace you?"

"I don't know." Mrs. Srivastava relaxed. "The union must know best . . . it has decided this after all."

"Who is the union?" I asked. "Who chooses the officers?"

She shrugged. "I don't know." She called out to the pharmacist, "Who is the union anyway?"

The pharmacist, the biggest flirt on the staff, leaned out of the window and yelled back, "How should I know? You think I'm a big shot?"

No one knew who the union was. No one knew the officers.

No one knew who had summoned them to strike. But they struck, because it said in the newspapers that they were striking.

We were concerned about the effect of the work stoppage on the hospital and turned up the first morning to see if we could help Dr. Agarwal. He had arrayed a long line of bottles on the table, and when he finished his usual one-minute examination of each patient he wrote out the prescription for us to dispense. He explained the code: "This is multi-vitamins, this one is an iron compound, this symbol means liver extract. AD capsules are the ones in the green can, the large pills are C vitamin, that mixture is cough syrup, this is aspirin . . ."

The bottles bore the blue and white label of UNICEF and manufacturing labels from Sweden, Yugoslavia, Denmark, or Italy. Almost all were vitamin or mineral pills. The hospital, the morning clinic with its long lines of sick patients, was operating as a gigantic dietary supplement, to make up for the lack of protein in village foods or to compensate for the ravages of hookworm on villagers who wore no shoes.

Now we understood how Dr. Agarwal could diagnose and treat sixty or seventy cases a day. He saw the same basic deficiency diseases over and over. We asked him about dietary education. He shook his head. He had tried it . . . they had done it in the army . . . but unlike soldiers the peasants and their wives did not have to take orders and had their own ideas about food. All his explanations had done was convince them that he was unwilling to prescribe proper medicines!

At the end of the day he thanked us and locked up. We felt that we had really done something, given someone something he wanted, something that in the short run would make him feel better.

In a day or two, however, some of the hospital staff drifted back and we were no longer needed. The rest of the staff stayed out another four or five days. Drinking tea with Mrs. Srivastava, I toyed with the idea of explaining that a union could be something more than a voice that called a strike through the newspaper. But could it really be? The union was plagued by the same rigidities that blocked communication within the Health Ministry. The same office clerks ran both and ran them in the same way: they sat at desks and handled files, and if they did not want something to happen they buried the file and said they couldn't find it. What happened in the union was an exact parallel to what had happened to Mrs. Srivastava's pay; the same insecurity prevented her from protesting in both cases. And she was tougher than most of the government staff.

The strike fizzled out. Gradually it dawned on the staff that the state government really did not have the money to pay them, but that it did not mind holding up their pay for a few weeks; it would help balance the budget. One by one the staff returned. Mrs. Dhan, the trained midwife from Tilaiya subcenter sauntered in and insisted that she had been sick for five days and had taken sick leave. Dr. Agarwal smiled and ordered the clerk to list her as "absent without leave from duty." Mandel claimed he had been working all along. Dr. Agarwal did not smile but ordered the same entry. Ratna Chakraverty, the midwife who had just come to work in Padma, said she had not even known about the strike until her father came to tell her. She had no radio of her own, did not read the paper, and the villagers had not considered the word of the strike gossip-worthy. She too lost her pay, though Judy was inclined to believe her.

The state government suspended the union, threatened to deprive the strikers of their pensions, and reported with satisfaction that the total stoppage of work by its entire civil service had "hardly disrupted the normal functioning of life." It was an odd boast but an honest one.

I finally decided that one thing I could do on my own, outside the system and without my mythical co-worker, was publicity. I had ordered two hundred posters from the Ministry of Health and Family Planning in New Delhi—bright yellow sheets with the red triangle symbolizing family planning and the slogan, "Do ya teen batche—bas!" ("Two or three children— enough!") To my amazement a postcard came saying that the posters had arrived at the railway station in Jhumri Tilaiya.

While I waited outside the dusty freight office, a peasant staggered into the waiting room, burdened with a huge jute bag which must have contained most of his household goods. He carefully lowered the bag to the floor, asked me to watch it for a moment, and still bent over, went to the window, approaching it from below out of respect. He kept his money scrunched up in the palm of his hand, below the counter. He wanted to see the ticket first, then he would show the ticket-seller that he had the cash to pay for it.

"One third-class ticket to Delhi."

"There is no train to Delhi today."

"Is there a train tomorrow?"

"Yes, there's one every day, but you've missed it."

The peasant turned away from the window, walked past me, stooped almost down to the floor, and hoisted up his parcel.

"Pardon father," I asked, "but don't you want to know what time the train leaves for Delhi tomorrow?"

He looked at me through his heavy glasses. "If God wishes, I will come in time. If not, there are other trains." He staggered off. I checked the timetable on the wall. He had missed the Delhi train by ten minutes.

I got my posters and carried them to the bus stop. As there were three buses waiting, I asked the dispatcher which would leave first for Barhi.

"When one of them leaves, I will tell you which bus goes first," he answered.

That was the way. A phone call to Hazaribagh was a gamble against dead lines, sleepy operators, wet equipment. An everyday conversation ran, "Namaste ji. I'm sorry I didn't make it yesterday."

"Oh, I didn't know. I couldn't come either."

I returned with my armload of posters but found I had no glue to put them up, so I stacked them on the shelf in our bedroom and a week later realized they were still there.

Even when I had a project that I was doing on my own, I too had to wait. Waiting in India is not, I was discovering, the same as being patient in America. Patience at home is needed when something expected takes longer than one had thought it would; it assumes that the bus will come or the project bear fruit. Waiting in India involves a suspension of expectation; something may or may not happen, the bus may never come.

I quit pushing my projects quite so hard. Push or no push, they didn't move. The posters grew mold during the monsoon.

In late July the rice in the paddy had been transplanted and now the terraced fields were hidden by the gentle green slopes of the grain. In Kariatpur Miss Sylvia smiled when we asked about the weather. She was still shy, but Chaudhuri laughed out loud as the water beat down on the tile roof of the health subcenter.

"Every peasant will be a king this year. Look at the paddy standing tall all around us. A good year."

Then the rains stopped and were replaced by a muggy heat, uncomfortable, but not as bad as May. No one seemed bothered; a few hot days were to be expected. The days stretched into a week, ten days. Slowly people began to worry about the weather. When would it rain again? As I pedaled through the villages old men pointed to the clouds and asked, "Will it rain today?" The paddies were still moist, but the standing water had dried up and in a few exposed areas the mud was covered with a thick layer of baked clay.

Attendance at the clinic dropped. "People are staying home to water wherever they can by hand," Dr. Agarwal said. "In another two weeks, if it doesn't rain, we'll lose the crop."

Mr. Kumar agreed. "A few fields have already lost some of their shoots. It's important in this season that the rain be regular, but it rarely is. We get enough water in Hazaribagh District, even too much, but at the wrong times. It's too hilly for irrigation, the water runs off quickly. If the paddy fails it will mean famine." The early maize crop had already failed because of the heavy rains in June.

Even Jagdish commented. "Prices have gone up again in the bazaar, sir. Last week rice was down to one rupee; now it's up to one and one-quarter. People are holding back; they're afraid of a drought." The peasants began murmuring about grain speculators. Inspectors raided Karu Sao's shop and found piled sacks of black-market grain.

The next time I visited Kariatpur, Chaudhuri was no longer laughing and Miss Sylvia looked sad. "It's very serious," she said. "Every day there are clouds and wind but no water. It is worse yet down the road." On my way back to Barhi I noticed that the biggest landowner in Kariatpur had his diesel pumps out irrigating his fields from the river. The drought would not hit all with equal force. By winter the poorer peasants would have to sell land to pay debts, and the landowner would need more diesel pumps to water his fields.

I fell into the grip of an incredible fear. Barhi was drifting into drought and a famine would follow and there was nothing I could do. Occasionally heavy clouds would form and a few drops would fall, scattering the dust. I would ride off cheerfully, expecting to be drenched, but the water did not come.

When I saw the mukhia or Mr. Kumar I tried to pin them down. How much longer could the paddy stand the dry weather? How long did we have for rain to save the crop? The mukhia guessed that although some paddies had already been lost, most could survive another two weeks, "if it's not too sunny." Mr. Kumar guessed a week. The fields still looked green to me, but the mud was a network of cracks. Only the lowest fields still gave off a damp swamp smell. The price of rice rose to one and one-half rupees. The poor began to eat maize and millet. Some owners gave up and let their goats graze off their crop.

No one could tell me if there would be a famine or not. No one knew how much time we had left. No one could say, "Well, if it doesn't rain by Tuesday, we'll have to get ready for famine relief."

It had been three weeks since a real rain. Judy and I went into Hazaribagh. We noticed that clouds had gathered over the ridges, but I concluded that they were what Jagdish called "bogus clouds." As we sat in a restaurant sipping coca-cola, a rush of cool air came in through the louvered windows at the top of the walls. The light in the room dimmed. We ran outside. Already the streets were half empty; rickshaw owners were hastily lifting up their canvas tops. It was not raining yet, but the clouds were black, then suddenly the muddy water was running off the streets and down the gutters. It was a reprieve! There was a month before harvest, and the crop could still fail, but for the moment everyone rejoiced. I thought of the old man in the railway station. I thought of our work, of our patient explanation that it was possible to decide now how many children you would want to have in a few years. I thought that I understood a little better why the word "planning" did not exist in the village dialect.

7. Judy and I returned one day from Hazaribagh to discover in our front yard a small puppy and a kitten, which neighborhood children had tied together by the legs. The animals were wailing piteously, the children watching, and I discovered I could manage a fairly presentable tongue lashing in Hindi. This was a sign that I was mastering the tongue, though Judy noted that I had bawled the children out in the respectful form of address. I reached down to untie the kitten, and as the knot was very tight, Judy brought me some scissors to cut the two terrified animals apart. Then I made the mistake of trying to pick up the kitten, to take it out of reach of the children. One small sharp fang sank into the center of my finger.

Rabies is endemic in India, and though the odds against a small kitten carrying the disease were astronomical, I would have to watch it for the ten-day incubation period anyway. Mumbling something about "damn nonsense" I scooped the kitten up, carried him whining into our bedroom, and sat down to figure out how to care for it. I was not sure it was even weaned.

We tried giving it milk. It refused to drink and mewed steadily throughout the afternoon and evening. As night fell we again tried to feed it, but it turned away, huddling under the bed. We went to sleep. About an hour later we heard the kitten's mother prowling outside in the courtyard. The kitten answered and scrambled over to the door. I was beginning to feel not at all humanitarian, and as the night wore on I began to convince myself that the kitten would never drink our milk, that it would die of starvation, that I would have to undergo rabies treatment, that the mother could take better care of the kitten anyway, that we could keep track of it by the bit of string still tied on its foot, and the best thing to do was to give it to its mother. About one o'clock we let it loose.

Faced with the problem of keeping track of the kitten, we hired some of the children to watch for us and report on the location of the nest. I didn't fully trust them, so every evening I would make sure that the mother was still nursing the kitten. For several days all went well. I was beginning to congratulate myself when, on the fourth day, the children reported that one kitten was missing. My heart sank. We could not find the mother. She had vanished. I questioned the boy who brought the news. It seemed that the kitten was not exactly missing. In fact, its father had snuck into the nest while the mother was away and had killed and eaten it. At first I did not believe it, but all the children in the neighborhood insisted that it had happened and that male cats often did this. The boy *thought* that the unfortunate kitten had not been the one with the string tied to it. The mother had fled to a safer lair.

I held off taking any action for that night hoping that we could find my kitten.

The following morning Bige, one of the boys who lived next door, beckoned me with his finger; he was looking at something lying in the path.

"The crows carried it here and dropped it," he said.

It was the hind leg of a small kitten, and tied around it was a piece of string.

So I went to Calcutta for a series of rabies shots, staying no longer than necessary in the muggy monsoon heat of Bengal, a heat that was little better than that of the summer. Shortly before 8 P.M. the day I left, I started for Howrah Station and the train ride back to Barhi. My train was scheduled to depart at 8:50.

Howrah Station must be the largest smoke-filled room in the world. If you stand still it seems smaller than Grand Central Station in New York because it is so packed with people. If you try to go anywhere it seems much larger, because it takes far longer to make your way through the ticket lines, the sweating baggage porters, the milling crowd, and the platform sleepers.

I had no reservation, so I hunted for the third-class ticket windows. Each window seemed to have swallowed the head of a great serpent which stretched around pillars and piles of luggage into the dark recesses of the station. Above each grill, gold lettering indicated the section of the line served. None of the names meant anything to me.

It was 8:20. Fighting down panic I asked a porter which window sold tickets for Tilaiya. He pointed to the end of a line which was not moving. A peasant and a policeman were just ahead of me. I asked what was going on. The peasant shrugged. The policeman turned around. "It's some fellow buying tickets for his company. Maybe fifty or sixty."

At 8:30 I asked the policeman if this was the right window for Tilaiya. He told me it was not, and pointed to one of the neighboring lines. This line was moving, slowly. Every few minutes someone would try to break in. The queue always repulsed the assault, but while the shouting was going on the ticket seller would pause to watch. I calmed myself with the thought that the train would be late.

Finally, at 9:00, I got my ticket. It had taken the seller a long time to find the cubbyhole for Tilaiya in the tall bank of destinations and longer to mark the revised fare on the cardboard label. I tried to run through the crowd; it was useless. The train had indeed left at 8:50.

The next train was 9:50. I settled down to wait, wishing that it was not so hot, wishing that I could make myself closely observe the life around me, wishing that I was on the train to Tilaiya.

About 9:15 headlights appeared far down the track and the crowds drifted to the outer end of the platform. The more agile moved to the very outer rim where they could jump into the first passing carriage and be sure of a window seat. I was inexperienced, so I waited about half way out, where the train would be moving a little more slowly. By the time the first third-class carriage passed, the train already looked full; arms and legs were coming out of doors, hands reached out windows to grab luggage left for safekeeping with a porter. Each carriage seemed more stuffed than the last. I jumped. The press of bodies in the entrance almost shoved me back onto the platform; I had to use my free elbow to get into the corridor. Inside a hundred skirmishes were taking place over seating space. Legs dangled from luggage racks. There was not room there to make a seven-hour trip in the heat. I made my way back to the platform and hunted up and down for a less crowded carriage.

I decided to try for a reserved seat. Seven or eight passengers were surrounding the conductor, all waving tickets and all, I supposed, trying to get the last reservation. I joined them. He spotted my white face and asked me what I wanted. I explained. He looked at my ticket, and looked puzzled. "But this has no reservation stamped on it!"

"I know. I'm trying to make one."

"But my dear friend, all of these people *have* reservations and I haven't got seats for them!"

It was back to the unreserved coaches, more jammed than before. I wasn't sure I would get in, but enough latecomers built up behind me and their shoving carried me to the end of a corridor. I looked for space to drop my sleeping bag, found none, and so stood holding it.

As the train gathered speed, my companions in the corridor made little adjustments to relieve the crush. An arm moved here, a leg there, and gradually almost everyone had a square foot or so in which to stand. I worked my way forward. The first compartment ran off to my left, and there seemed to be room for me amidst the bundles on the luggage rack.

Carefully removing my sandals and slipping them under the wooden seat, I hoisted myself onto the rack and began to rearrange the bundles to provide a flat surface for sitting.

From underneath my foot a harsh voice barked, "Don't move that luggage." I started and peered down, but the speaker's face was hidden.

"I won't hurt them. I just want a place to sit."

"Luggage racks are for luggage. Leave them be." I looked around me. Every other luggage rack was carrying two or three passengers. The speaker's tone of voice might have been unexceptional on a New York City bus, but I had never encountered such hostility in India. I was tired, hot, and resentful. Here I was traveling third class because I did not want special treatment, removing my sandals to comply with the prohibition against touching anyone with leather, humbly imitating the other luggage-rack danglers. And I was met with what, by Indian standards, was extraordinary rudeness.

Ignoring the man's last remark, I moved his luggage the bare minimum necessary to clear a six-inch ledge. I perched my rump, propped myself up with one hand, and lay back against the luggage.

Another voice sounded from below. "Don't sit like that. You're leaning on my luggage. Sit up straight."

The luggage in question was a burlap bag filled with rice. I felt close to tears but tried to sit upright, which required that I lean over the corridor, hold on to the overhead fan with one hand and to the opposite luggage rack with the other. I could not have held this position long, but at the moment I was more worried about the attacks from below.

Just then a voice on the opposite seat suggested, "Leave him alone, brothers. Where is he to sit?" Neither of my persecutors replied. Feeling justified, I leaned back a little. At any other time it would have seemed unbearably uncomfortable, but here it had the advantage of being not quite painful, and I gratefully accepted what was allowed.

The train pulled into Burdwan, the first stop. I could see bodies crawling out of windows after their luggage. No one could reach the doors. I understood why third-class carriages, unlike first- and second-class ones, had no bars on the windows. But what about the passengers waiting to get on the train at Burdwan? One or two had crashed their way through the nearest door, but surely there were others?

There were. A heavy rucksack flew in the window of our compartment. Two hands grasped the edge of the window and a man tried to lift himself into our carriage. A passenger next to the window shouted at him, "No, *bhai*. No room in this car. Try another."

"All the cars are full. Let us in," came the reply. The passengers beneath me picked up the intruder's sack and forced it out the window into his chest. He lurched back on the platform. The whistle sounded. Silently I was rooting for him, imagining his desperation. Once again he tried to get in. By now the train had begun to move. This time not even the luggage made it. The window slammed down, leaving a voice yelling at us from the platform.

Each station produced a similar incident. Now the first effort to storm the window was met by slamming it shut. At one station a passenger got out. Someone, figuring that this meant room for one new body, tried to get in. He had the sense to climb in before his luggage. But the other passengers were not willing to agree with the theory that there was more room. The newcomer turned and reached out the window to get his pack from the platform. The passengers tried to grab his arm, but he pulled the light suitcase in. Then the train moved, and everyone sat back.

I no longer felt personally hurt by the attack at the start of the trip. I was lucky the violence had only been verbal. I understood the reason for the fighting: there might not be another train, and if there was, it was unlikely to be less crowded; on the other hand the crowded passengers were suffering terribly in the heat.

The only human conditions were in the reserved carriages. But it would have been ludicrous to make all cars reserved. Only half the passengers could have made it in official spaces; the others had to be squeezed in where there was no room but where room might somehow be made.

Yet the railroads ran all the cars the tracks could accommodate. The trip and the relief which set in once I got out into the cool, open spaces of the Tilaiya railroad station put my mind back on population. The crowded train was a microcosm of the crowding I had carefully skirted in Calcutta. And now I could see how the common courtesy, the humanity, even the passivity of Barhi could yield to a destructive frenzy. The thought was uncomfortable. I had been reconciling myself to the inevitability of the inertia that held Barhi in poverty. But how fragile that small cushion of security was! Surely one could do *something,* make some contribution. People had welcomed us, even if we had not always been able to understand or communicate. We had said that we meant to help, and so far we had not. I did not know what I was going to do, I would never know in advance what would work. But I had to look for an opening.

Jagdish gave us the opening. His wife had given birth to a boy in February, their first child. Jagdish asked Judy if she would tell him about caring for the boy so that he could be "strong and healthy, just like Sahib." At that moment I weighed 115 pounds and was suffering from minor dysentery. In any case Judy told Jagdish about nutrition and reminded him that after the first four months mother's milk was not sufficient. The advice was intended to show that we cared. Jagdish carried the word home with him, but we had seen how little effect advice from men had on the mothers of Barhi. Even Dr. Agarwal was unable to control his own wife's diet during pregnancy.

So Judy was quite pleased at the start of the monsoon when Jagdish reported that the baby was eating some banana at four months. Now, in August, the baby was six months old. "You should see the baby, Memsahib. We have been feeding it just as you said, spinach, and mashed fruits, and boiled lentils."

"How is he doing?" Judy asked. "Does he like the food?"

"Oh, yes, Memsahib," Jagdish said, smiling. "And he's so healthy and strong. So much energy that my wife complains, 'How can I take care of such a baby!' It's always kicking and screaming, making trouble." He laughed. "The neighbors think it's so difficult to have such a strong baby. But a few have asked my wife what she does, and Lalita Devi has begun to feed her baby other foods."

"And the rest?" I asked.

He laughed. "Oh, they say all that food makes a baby sick. But I just point and say, 'Is that baby sick?' All those women are so ignorant."

Jagdish had instructed his wife not because he understood why but because he trusted us. Mainly by providing him with vitamins during his colds, we had shown that we could help; this, combined with Jagdish's amazing openness, had proved strong enough to overcome the conservatism of the women.

It seemed possible that trained midwives like Miss Sylvia might build trust if they carried vitamin supplements for infants into the field with them. This might give the meetings some importance to the mothers in the village and convince them to begin using trained midwives for deliveries, instead of their traditional village "chamains." And convincing the women to use contraception, Judy knew, hung on getting them to make this switch.

She broached the subject cautiously to Dr. Agarwal.

"If we do that," he told her, "none of the women will come to the subcenters, and it would be very difficult to maintain proper records in the field."

Judy did not point out that none of the women came anyway; it was the second reason that overrode her suggestion.

But we were not ready to give up that easily. We thought we

knew what needed to be done, but we still had to find someone with whom to do it. And, as if by miracle, rumors began to fly that a new Lady Doctor was coming to Barhi. Dr. Agarwal refused to believe it. "Barhi's too small, no one will ever come here."

Someone did. We arrived at the hospital one morning and found Dr. Agarwal talking to Dr. Kamla Malik and her husband, also a physician, who would shortly be going to England for advanced degree work.

Judy guessed from the sari she was wearing that Dr. Malik was a Bengali, not a Bihari. She was right, but Dr. Malik explained that her father lived in Hazaribagh and that she had grown up in Bihar. She and Dr. Agarwal made arrangements for her to take over direct supervision of the family planning staff. Dr. Agarwal, of course, would still be available to do vasectomies and for other work where a man was necessary. But the onus of supervision, bookkeeping, and records passed to the new doctor.

Judy now had someone who could insert the loops and give the necessary post-insertion care to the women on a regular basis. I was pleased too. Dr. Malik was more at ease with us than was Dr. Agarwal, and we hoped she would be less caught up in official routines. Perhaps she would get the staff to do more and record less.

Building hopes from our one experience with Jagdish, Judy and I plotted. We would not worry so much about the family planning message but would stress the family planning messenger's task of building trust in the villages.

Of course, there was still Mandel. I did not trust him and couldn't imagine why a villager would. He didn't like Barhi. But I had heard very good things about my Block Extension Educator, Ram Sewak Sinha, who worked as a Health Worker in the southern part of the block. And now that Dr. Malik had come, perhaps I could convince Ram Sewak Sinha to give up that post and join us in Barhi. If he had been a Health Worker, there was a good chance that he knew how to earn the confidence of village families.

Champadih, the village where Ram Sewak worked, was eight miles from Barhi. We would visit him and persuade him to come to Barhi immediately. So once again Dr. Agarwal, Dr. Malik, Judy and I, the pharmacist, and the ward attendant, all crowded into the jeep and lurched off. A jeep ride always made Barhi seem exciting. We would swerve off the road onto the shoulder to get out of the way of an overladen truck, screech to a halt to avoid hitting a water buffalo, then accelerate again through a mud-colored village whose women hid their faces from us. And there was always the unknown: "Will the jeep break down?"

The transmission, the carburetor, and the battery were in good health that afternoon, and in half an hour we scraped through a narrow path bounded by high thorn hedges and came out into the middle of a mango grove. A small building at the eastern end bore a sign designating the Bihar State Health Department, Champadih Village Health Center.

Champadih rested at the foot of the line of hills that marked the boundaries of Barhi Block. In front of the health center was a pasture. Nothing had been planted on it; it was a blessed expanse of wildflowers and grass, the first such open field I had seen since coming to Barhi.

High clouds lay piled up over the hills. It was still the monsoon season, and the land took on great beauty from the sky. I was feeling good.

Dr. Agarwal was supposed to visit this subcenter every week to handle the more serious cases which were beyond Ram Sewak's skill. But the government did not allow him enough money to buy gasoline for the jeep, and when he did have gasoline money the jeep was usually being repaired. Dr. Agarwal had not been here in several months, so there were many cases.

Dr. Agarwal examined the patients. Only one was serious—an old man with an abscessed tooth. Dr. Agarwal give him aspirin, enough for two days, and told him to go to Hazaribagh to have it removed. The old man wanted a shot to relieve the pain, and more pills. Dr. Agarwal refused. He explained that if he gave the man painkillers he would not go to Hazaribagh, and the abscess would grow worse. When he had finished with the cases, he told me I could have my talk with Ram Sewak Sinha.

Ram Sewak was in the rear of the dark dispensary room, storing brown bottles and blue-and-white tins of UNICEF vitamins in a sagging wooden cabinet. I had met him at monthly meetings. He was big, stocky, with a broad face, close-clipped iron grey hair and a peasant's solid presence. This was a real person in front of me, unlike so many government clerks who seemed insubstantial, less real than the furniture of their offices. He turned around when my body blocked out the light from the doorway. "Namaste, Sahib."

"Namaste, Sinha Sahib. Can we talk?"

He came outside and we sat down on the steps.

"When do you think you will come to Barhi?" I asked.

"When someone comes to replace me. Frankly, I'm in no hurry." He looked at me carefully. "I don't want to shift to family planning. Here in Champidah I have a position of respect. I have a good private practice which yields three or four hundred rupees a month. I am responsible for a five-mile area. Once I come to Barhi, to work in family planning, I lose that status, I lose that income, and I have to go riding on my bicycle all over the block. All this for an extra twenty rupees a month. Of course, I have to do it sometime. It's the order. But why hurry?"

I was prepared to answer him. "Well, I understand your problem. But family planning is important to this area, it's important to India. And the government has asked you to help with that work here in Barhi. The program needs you. But in any case, as you say, you'll have to join eventually. I thought we could talk about what we would do after you come."

He thought. "The big thing is night halts. We have all these subcenters to supervise—Kariatpur, Garukhura, Tilaiya Dam, Gauriakarma, Champadih, and some of them are a long way from Barhi. Tilaiya Dam is fifteen miles. We'll have to go overnight to do anything." He looked out at the pasture. "The regulations say that the Extension Educator has to make seven night halts each month."

I didn't answer. I had little enthusiasm for the regulations. I could tell that he was concerned about the cost of the night halts, but I was more impressed by the fact that he seemed to be taking the work seriously. It would never have occurred to me to ask Mandel to make a night halt—least of all to ask him to do so because regulations required it. I did not know how many night halts Ram Sewak would end up making with me, but the prospect, after eight months in Barhi, seemed almost visionary.

I looked at Ram Sewak. He didn't look like a visionary. Before parting, we agreed that I would come the next week and go along with him on his public health visits to the villages. He was doing a final check of the children in the area to see that all had been vaccinated.

The day I spent with Ram Sewak was quite a contrast to the chaotic flight of the villagers in Kariatpur from the smallpox innoculation team, as Judy had described it. Ram Sewak *attracted* children; even the giggling women behind their saris responded to his presence. He could ask them about the health of their children, look at their runny eyes, gossip about their neighbors, sympathize with a recent death in the family; he could do all this because he knew these people as individuals. I had almost forgotten that it was possible for medicine to be personal. But I could see the results. The people trusted his deep voice and let him reach out and turn up the forearms of their children to see if they had been innoculated against smallpox. The children, usually terrified of a strange touch, stood quietly while he did this.

The doors that had opened to Ram Sewak in Champadih had first opened in an epidemic, but he had known how to keep them open. I was a little concerned that he would not be able to open them as family planning worker for the entire block. But the two of us would have to find a way.

When I next came to Champadih, Ram Sewak suggested we visit Barisal, one of the poorest villages nearby, to talk to the people and see how they lived. It crossed my mind that Ram Sewak was trying to please me by following suggestions I had given at Dr. Agarwal's request to the uncomprehending medical staff at the monthly meetings. But how had he remembered those suggestions, how had he separated them in his mind from the welter of instructions Dr. Agarwal delivered each month in the form of "orders"?

We walked the half mile from Champadih to the main road between Barhi and Hazaribagh, went a hundred yards along the road, then turned down a narrow path toward a cluster of houses perched in the middle of paddy fields. I asked Ram Sewak why he thought the villagers would be at home; it was midafternoon and almost everyone should have been in the fields. He explained that these were not peasants; these people made the bamboo baskets and mats that were sold in the bazaar on market days.

As we approached, I could see a small number of men, women, and children working in the open area between the houses. Ram Sewak had not exaggerated their poverty. The women wore no bangles. In Barhi the rich wore eighteen-carat gold, the middle class wore fourteen-carat gold, the ordinary peasant's wife wore elaborate hollow silver, and the poor wore glass. Glass bangles sold in the bazaar for twelve or fifteen to the rupee. Everyone, I had thought, could afford that. But no one in Barisal was wearing a single glass bangle. Except for the crude mud huts, the stacks of completed baskets, the bamboo used in making the baskets, and the basket tools themselves, there was nothing in the village. There were no agricultural tools. No one had planted any of the climbing gourds and beans that most people used to supplement their diet. There were no extra clothes hanging from the rafters of the houses to dry; no piles of cookingware set in the sun after washing; no buckets, no tins for carrying water, no chairs, no string beds, no padlocks on the doors.

The people were thin and haggard. Several of the young children had the bleached hair that marks protein malnutrition; the teeth of even the young women were very bad.

Why were they so poor? There always seemed to be a good market for the baskets at market day, and they usually sold for about one-half rupee. Four or five baskets thus brought as much income as the usual day laborer earned, and they did not look very complicated to make.

I asked Ram Sewak and all he said was, "They are as poor as they seem. Ask them why they grow no vegetables." An old man, but perhaps he only looked old, glanced up from plaiting the thin bamboo strips. "How could we have vegetables. We own no land. Even the land these houses are on belongs to the peasants of Kariatpur. We are not allowed vegetables. We must buy from the peasants in the bazaar."

He went back to his bamboo strips. I began to suspect that Ram Sewak's reason for coming here had been not to please me but to test me. He wanted to see if I, like the other sahibs he had known, British and Indian, would be too terrified of this poverty to go out to the villages.

An old woman squatted over a section of bamboo about twelve feet long and whittled away at it with a curved knife which she held between her hands, the edge facing her, and pulled towards her feet. I assumed she was preparing it for further splitting. She continued to whittle. The bamboo was hard, and each time she pulled the knife towards her only a thin sliver peeled off.

She was still whittling on the same two-foot section ten minutes later. I realized that she would not split the bamboo again. She was whittling the section down to the thinness of one of the strands woven into a basket, to perhaps a fifth of its original size. Only in this way would the rigid bamboo become flexible enough to be woven. I was fascinated and sickened. Thinking of the hundred or so strands in each basket and of the hours that it took this woman to prepare that bamboo for weaving, and of the half-rupee that someone—probably a middleman—would get for selling it, and of how little she could buy with whatever she got, I wondered how or why anyone in the village survived. What was the point in trying to convince these people to limit the number of their children? They would not benefit if they did. Next to the woman a young girl was plaiting the finely whittled strips into the graceful shape of a wide basket. The green, shiny, outer covering of the bamboo formed a pleasing pattern with the white, fibrous surfaces exposed by the whittling. The baskets were among the most attractive things sold in the market, and I had always felt cheered seeing them in their tall stacks.

I glanced at Ram Sewak, who was sitting quietly, looking grave. His point about Barisal had been made. He got up and walked over to each of the basket weavers, leaned down and thanked them individually for letting us watch their skill. We gestured namaste and went silently back to the main road.

"When I leave, Pope Sahib," he asked me when we got to the subcenter, "where will those people go when they are sick?"

"To the health worker who replaces you," I said.

He nodded. "But at first they won't trust him. Still, I know that family planning is needed. Thirty years ago the peasants did not grind those people as hard. There was enough land then for everyone to have a small garden and there was enough work for every hand. So I'll come to work with you in Barhi. But it's not easy."

I smiled at him. I knew that he was upset because he had not sorted out his reasons for wanting to stay in Champadih. He had a private practice among the wealthy peasants, and he could help the poor; but he didn't know which interest dominated. He told me that he would join us as soon as a replacement came, and I rode back to Barhi to see how Judy's work with Dr. Kamla Malik was going.

I had been with Judy at the hospital on the first day that Dr. Malik planned to insert loops. Judy had been apprehensive about Dr. Malik's medical technique. Another doctor's sloppy work had caused a great many complications among the women, and this had given the loop a bad reputation. We had seen Dr. Malik approaching that day, her umbrella held up against the sun. She had looked back at the road, obviously proud at having walked the two hundred yards from her house. "Is Mrs. Srivastava, the public health nurse, here?" she inquired, "Is everything ready?"

"Yes, Memsahib," Mrs. Srivastava's high voice sounded from inside the hospital. "Everything is ready."

Dr. Malik went inside and a minute later I saw Mrs. Srivastava out on the back porch resterilizing all the instruments.

Dr. Malik was everything Judy had wished for. She cared about medical techniques and about the program. She did not care for paperwork. With Dr. Usha Narayin it had all been papers, records, service books, accounts, stock ledgers, tour diaries, monthly reports, indent forms, pay books, and loop registers that were jumbled, missing, or incorrect. Dr. Malik calmly turned the whole cupboard of documents over to the clerk, and told him that she would not take charge until he made sense out of them. The clerk bought a brand-new padlock and locked the cupboard. Dr. Malik opened a fresh set of all the accounts she was required to keep.

Judy had found, and I had almost found, a real co-worker, someone who could go about the business of family planning with a good deal more intelligence than two Americans. It had taken nine months, and it was the one thing the Peace Corps was supposed to have checked on before it sent us.

Strolling in the bazaar during the first week in September, I heard a deep voice calling out, "Oh, Pope Sahib, oh Pope Sahib." I turned around. Ram Sewak was sitting in one of the wooden chairs in the barber shop, his back to me, his hair edged with shaving soap, his eyes glinting from the mirror on the wall.

"I'll be at the tea stall," I told him. "Come when you're finished and I'll buy you a cup."

He joined me shortly. "Special tea, bearer," he instructed, "for me and the Sahib. They have two varieties here. I wanted to make sure we got the first-class kind. You can buy next time."

"Do you always come to Barhi to have your hair cut?"

"Oh, no. There is a good barber in Champadih. No, I moved into Barhi yesterday, as I promised you. My replacement has come."

"That's good news . . . for me at least. How do you feel?"

He was unhappy, he admitted, about losing his private practice. I asked if he had considered trying to bribe the clerks in Hazaribagh to stop his transfer. He looked very pained: "I am in government service. I take what comes." We agreed to go out the next morning to the village of Rasoiya Dhamna, about two miles from Barhi. Ram Sewak knew the mukhia, and thought he might be helpful.

The mukhia did help. He greeted my new co-worker and me cordially and assembled eight or ten men and a handful of children under the shade of the veranda for a meeting. The mukhia stood against a pillar, Ram Sewak and I sat on a cot. The mukhia, I noted, had carefully taken a position where he could mediate between the government and the village, instead of sitting next to us as Ram Sewak had suggested.

Ram Sewak spent about ten minutes sweeping imaginary straw off the cot while the men settled down on their haunches and began sucking twigs. When it was quiet, Ram Sewak began.

"Let's talk about your families," he said, "let's think about their needs. How can we feed them? How can we educate them? How can we find work for our sons and marry our daughters? Sahib and I have come to help you answer these questions."

Ram Sewak explained that family planning meant controlling children, that this was the purpose of the operation that a few men from Dhamna had had in Barhi during the famine. He asked if the men understood, and inevitably one old man tried to put Ram Sewak down. "But Sahibs, aren't children the gift of God?"

"Of course they are God's gift. But we decide when. Look, if we don't put seeds in the field, will we harvest a crop? If you don't plant potatoes, can you harvest them?"

The mukhia arbitrated. No seed, no crop, he decided. Everyone looked relieved.

"Well," Ram Sewak went on, "it's the same with children. If you don't plant your seed, there won't be children. Right?"

The men smiled and shook their heads. "No seed, no crop,

Sahib is very wise," said an old man in a cracked voice, "very wise. But," he pointed to his stomach, "my planting days are done, Sahib. What is all this to me?"

"What is done is done. But think of the future. If there are so many mouths and no more land, how will we feed them? And you, father, should explain this to your children."

"Oh, yes," said the old man, exaggerating the nod of his head to emphasize the vigor of his commitment to family planning, "I'm always telling them. But in my youth there was no family planning problem! Sahib there wouldn't know why." Several of the other old men cackled. The mukhia looked serious. "Times are very corrupt, Sahib," the old man said to me. "In this village, this very village, men and women are living together—alone! Sleeping together whenever they like . . . even in the daytime! I lived with my parents. One room for all the men, one for the women, and one for . . . for doing it. My mother *knew* what was going on. Not like today. That's why we have so many children. Stop *that*, Sahib, and you will solve the problem!"

I waited for Ram Sewak to respond. He evaded the issue. Times had changed, he explained. Now big doctors, important men, tell us how we can plough the field without planting the seed. This was the vasectomy. In the big cities, rich men waited in line and paid doctors one hundred rupees for doing this wonderful operation. The rich men knew that small families were better. Look at the Raja of Ramgarh, the political boss of the district, the old landlord. He had only one son. Now the government was ready to offer this same operation to everyone, free. In fact they would give you twenty-five rupees.

The men agreed. Of course the government was their mother and father, and very generous to offer family planning doctors to poor people. But they had heard that family planning was only for Hindus, that the Muslims did not believe in it, and that if the Hindus only had the operation, there would soon be more Muslims.

Ram Sewak denied it, mentioned Muslim villages where men had had the operation, and said that if the Muslims did not plan their families they would be the losers. Look at what had happened to the fields the last two generations. Where once a man owned enough to feed his family and to store food against bad years, now the land was so badly divided that even an ordinary harvest meant hunger for most people. The pasture had all been plowed up and now there was not enough milk even for the children to drink. Family planning would make Hindus richer and stronger, not weaker.

"Whatever you say, Sahib," the mukhia said. "We will talk to the men who are having too many children. But right now it is the busy season in the fields. Our men will come for the operation in the cold season. Twenty-five rupees is what the government gives?"

Ram Sewak explained that in addition to the twenty-five rupees, all the medicines and care were free. The mukhia thanked us for coming, we thanked him for calling the meeting, and we left the old men sitting on the ground, still gossiping about the corruption and immorality of the times, especially of the young women who lived alone with their husbands.

8. Twice a year the government ordained a "Family Planning Fortnight" during which agencies of the government would be our allies. In practice, Dr. Agarwal explained, the family planning program existed in most blocks only during these periods. Dr. Agarwal set up a schedule of staff meetings for the last two weeks of September and arranged to tour the villages at the end of the fortnight's propaganda activities to perform vasectomies and give other medical services. I was looking forward to collaborating with Ram Sewak.

The first morning of the fortnight I heard the spinning gears of a bicycle come to a halt before the front porch. "Oh, Pope Sahib," Ram Sewak's voice bellowed, "Are you ready?"

"Of course," I yelled. I grabbed up my yellow canteen of water, a burlap bag with a dozen bananas, a set of flash cards on reproductive anatomy, and a dozen condoms for demonstration purposes.

We were to cycle to Tilaiya Dam, inspect the work of Olivia Dhan, the trained midwife, then on to the village of Kohlua Kahlan to conduct a mass meeting. Ram Sewak pointedly remarked that it was seventeen miles to Kohlua Kahlan. "You can't say I don't work, Pope Sahib." I agreed; he worked harder than anyone else. I asked him where he picked up the habit.

"That's just how I am." On the way out of town he stopped to consult the pharmacist Nagu Sao. I gathered that Ram Sewak was trying to drum up some private medical practice in Barhi, but Barhi already had a state hospital and two pharmacists. Ram Sewak also hoped to be transferred back to his health subcenter since officially his transfer was temporary. I would have been astounded if the dhoti-clad clerks in Hazaribagh, who had taken six months to move the file on his original transfer, would undo it any faster. For one thing, his salary as a family planning worker came from the central government. If he returned to health work, the state, that is Hazaribagh, would have to pay him. That alone would cause Dr. Gope to hesitate before signing any transfer order.

After the chat with Nagu Sao, Ram Sewak strode out to his bicycle, mounted, and rode off towards Tilaiya Dam, pajama cuffs flapping. The wind was stiffening the Hanuman flag over the temple; it would be pushing against us all the way to the dam. But then the wind always pushed against us. I was becoming an animist; the Wind God was opposed to family planning.

The first long hill wasn't bad: a rocky red slope sheltered us from the worst gusts. After clattering over the rough pavement at the top we drifted down steep curves toward the lake itself, barely able to coast, for the wind rounded the curves ahead of us, always with its powerful breath blowing against my chest.

We paused at the tea stall where a narrow road to the dam turned off the main highway. It was the sleepiest tea stall in the area, though it doubled as a village shop for the handful of houses nearby. The Punjabi truck drivers stopped here only in the summer, when they would strip to shorts and wade into the waters of the lake. The rest of the year the tea stall served the handful of bus passengers who walked to the dam from here or, loaded with goods, waited for the one cycle rickshaw which plied the road.

The tea was muddy, the wind was getting stronger. An occasional dust devil swirled down the road and vanished as it passed over the brown water about fifty yards away. A water buffalo tied at the back of the tea stall chewed randomly on a bamboo screen wall, its tail slowly brushing the flies from its hollow flanks.

I gulped down my tea and reclined against the screen, cooled on the outside by the beads of sweat induced by drinking the hot liquid. We had had some rain in September, not enough to insure a bumper harvest but enough to ward off famine. As the monsoon receded, the heat had returned.

Ram Sewak drank steadily, feet tucked under his legs, eyes watching the thin road toward the dam. I did not understand how he could face the glare without squinting. He considered my sun glasses an affectation and a weakness. Finally, he handed the proprietor forty paise in light aluminum coins. "Shall we go, brother?"

We turned down the road, the wind tugged at my loose clothing, and soon my legs felt as though they were pushing the pedals through thick mud. I had to squint to keep a fuzzy view of the pavement. Several times as we rounded bends I wanted to get off and give up. But I knew it was no use. As we turned around, the wind turned with us. Ram Sewak outweighed me, two to one, an advantage for me when we had to cycle up a hill, but now a handicap. His legs pumped the pedals faster than mine. Ahead, a low forest of bamboo and cashew offered the only windbreak on the five miles between the highway and the dam. Today, however, the gusts roared down the passage between the yellow-green leaves and the barbed wire fencing, ruffling the bamboo and bending the cashew branches. At the three-mile mark I gave out, ran my bike drunkenly into the ditch and shoved my sandal onto the white marker to balance it. Ram Sewak circled and, catching the wind, drifted back. "Rest?"

"Rest," I assented. We set the bikes on their kickstands and lay in the shade of the bamboo with our heads against the bank. "Insane," I said.

"What's insane?"

"All this." I waved at the bicycle, the road, the windy branches. I stripped the sweat off my cheek and flicked it off my fingers. "Dr. Gope should be here."

"Dr. Gope would die if he had to do this. Can't you convince the government to give us a motorcycle for this work?"

"Who, me? The ministry is already tired of the Peace Corps Volunteers trying to improve the conditions of the staff. They'd like to send us home. I'll ask . . . but don't expect anything."

Ram Sewak looked at the leaves, indicated that the wind had died and that it was time to go. I brushed off my shorts, jerked the bike up from the dust where it had fallen, and we soon reached the top of the grade. I propped my feet up on the frame and coasted to the foot of the dam. The water was high under the sluice gates, so we couldn't use the stepping stones. We climbed the winding road to the top of the dam, walked our cycles over it, and on the other side mounted again. Jouncing over a shepherd's path that threatened at any moment to dump us, we reached the huge peepal tree at the edge of Tilaiya, where Olivia Dhan worked. Pedaling into the village we scattered a handful of chickens that had taken refuge from the sun under the tree.

I had been here once before, with Dr. Agarwal, but couldn't remember which of the large mud houses was the subcenter. Ram Sewak got directions from a young peasant working in his garden, and we found the small red triangle which told us we had arrived. The one-room center had no window and was locked except when the doctor came. Olivia Dhan herself shared quarters with one of the widows in the village.

She greeted us at the wooden doorway, warned us to duck our heads, and seated us on a cot. The veranda was taken up with cots, aluminum pots and pans stacked for airing, and drying laundry.

While Mrs. Dhan prepared tea, Ram Sewak whispered that the villagers were quite unhappy about her. She had become "very good friends" with the agricultural worker. I had heard the rumors. Of course Ram Sewak had expected it, he didn't seem to disapprove. Mrs. Dhan's husband was posted several hundred miles away in accordance with time-honored Government of Bihar practice. How could she not get involved with another man. After all, women had sixteen times as much sexual desire as men. I questioned this startling statistic. He looked at me as if to say, "Don't you even know that?"

Ram Sewak explained that the woman was the aggressor and the one who benefitted from sex. The man should give in only often enough to keep his wife faithful, because every drop of semen he lost weakened him in mind and body. The replacement of a drop of semen required four drops of blood.

I knew that Ram Sewak had three years of training as a paramedical and was familiar with anatomy and physiology, so I was stunned by these misconceptions.

Then Ram Sewak questioned me. He seemed astonished that I did not accept one act of intercourse per month as the moral-sexual ideal, that I did not find it impossible to imagine that Mrs. Dhan could have resisted the agricultural worker, and that in general most of the folk beliefs I held about sex were totally opposed to his.

He concluded that American women must be different. I tossed in the idea that perhaps it was how people were brought up. Ram Sewak paused. To his own belief in the relatively inexhaustible libido of women, he now had to add my idea of the sexually aggressive man. As a moralist, he explained, he could only deplore this. Things were bad enough in Bihar, where women were always looking for new partners. But if the men also began straying . . . why everyone would destroy his mind and body in mass orgies.

I think he was relieved when Mrs. Dhan brought the tea and put an end to the discussion. She handed Ram Sewak two dog-eared registers and asked him to check them. I took one and leafed through it idly. Ram Sewak browsed through the other; he looked unhappy. Finally he called her over and pointed to the columns. The register was not in the proper form at all. Why didn't she use the models provided by Dr. Agarwal at the monthly meetings?

Her eyes flashed, she raised her hands to heaven. "You may be able to follow the doctor, Sinha Sahib, but how can I? He always uses English words, who knows what they mean?" She tightened the sash of her sari defiantly.

Dr. Agarwal's patient explanations invariably had shifted into English. Records had always been kept in English. I supposed that the ideas they contained had been learned in English and the procedures for keeping them were English. I doubted that Dr. Agarwal could think about recordkeeping in Hindi and was sure that many of the headings which fitted the columns so neatly in English would demand ponderous phrases and half-paragraph descriptions in Hindi.

These records bore no relationship to the work in the field; the language barrier symbolized this division. The staff had two jobs. They went out to the villages, talked to a few people, added a little information about family planning to the small tradition of village bore, and came back to insure that this new bit of knowledge imbedded itself in the circular movement of opinion. This was the vernacular job. Ram Sewak was good at it because he could wrap up new ideas in the old ones about crops and rain, father and son, men and gods. And, although it was harder for me, this was what Judy and I had come to do. The audio-visual aids we prepared for the staff were designed to compensate for the abstract nature of the idea of "nonpregnancy." The schedules we set up were intended to reinforce the new ideas by repeated presentations. Our appeals to higher authorities in the Health Ministry were aimed at getting them to recognize and appreciate family planning.

But the Health Ministry was obsessed by the other job, the English job, which involved the use of registers and files. The staff recorded regular visits to selected target couples, conducted surveys, persuaded individual families to adopt some methods of family planning, and in general carried out the latest scientific directives of the state or district family planning officials. Since every directive was arranged around some new bit of book-keeping, the staff could only interpret the order through the records demanded as a result of it. Their ability to satisfy their superiors depended on their ability to keep these records.

Since most of the staff members were from the villages, they might have been able to play the vernacular role. But that required enthusiasm and morale, and the Bihar state government viewed morale as a noxious weed. Since work is bad for people, they reasoned, anyone who appears to enjoy it must not be doing it. So no one in authority was willing to make the staff members *want* to do the first job. Instead they compelled them, through fear, to try to do the second. Unfortunately, the second job could not be expressed at all in the village Hindi which was all that most of the staff could use. Dr. Agarwal fell back on English—and mystified the staff.

So far only Ram Sewak of all the field workers I had met had resolved this dilemma. His strength, oddly, was that he had a very limited knowledge of English, just enough to get him through paper work but not enough to confuse him about what the work was. He had a shrewd integrity. He was a peasant. Unlike Mandel, he liked the village world. He respected its insistence on the nonliterate tradition, shared its prejudices (as on sex) even where they conflicted with his medical training. He saw himself as supplementing village tradition and its prejudices with a few new, necessary ideas about health and family planning which he had learned in English books. He was the ideal translator.

I wondered if he could show Mrs. Dhan how to mediate

between the two tasks. He gave her one of his own registers and told her to copy the columns he had made. He showed her how to insert one sheet at the back so that it stuck above the other pages. By writing column titles on that one sheet, she could save the labor of writing them on every sheet. He checked her registers, found that she was entering all the right data but in the wrong places.

"Of course I am, Sinha Sahib. I know my job. It's just the registers that confuse me." She was still angry.

Ram Sewak soothed her by praising her work and assuring her that it was only on paper that she was not meeting the doctor's requirements. His good will was clear. Finally they both laughed, and we finished the visit with talk about the weather and her tea. She took the praise with a coy smile. I thought of myself as a village worker making my daily rounds in these isolated places. The agricultural extension worker had good taste.

Outside, the wind was waiting for us. Ram Sewak pedaled off ahead of me in the direction of Kohlua Kahlan, and for about one and one-half hours we pushed on over a rough dirt road which impressed every foot of its profile on my rear. We passed no village, only rugged hills and plateaus scarred by erosion and held down by the scrawniest of thorn bushes. My breath came in shorter and shorter gasps, and finally I signaled to Ram Sewak to stop. He pulled over. I took the bag off my cycle and asked him if he would like to share a bunch of bananas.

"You have bananas with you, Pope Sahib? Why didn't you tell me before! Here we are, practically starving, dying of exhaustion, and you don't even tell me that you have bananas. One dozen!" He shifted briefly into elaborate schoolboy English. "You are my very good friend, Mr. Pope."

We both felt better after the bananas, although neither of us had much confidence that we were really headed for Kohlua Kahlan. We set off anyway, to the accompaniment of a rising wind. If I had been alone I would have turned back. Ram Sewak took up an unmelodic chant: "Kohlua KAHLAN! KOHLUA Kahlan! Kohlua KAHLAN! KOHLUA Kahlan!" This somehow expressed my resolve not to worry, not to let my brain complain about my exhaustion, to act like one of a pair of happy madmen, working hard and going nowhere. I was not as short of breath once I joined Ram Sewak in wasting it on singing.

106

We did get to Kohlua Kahlan, an accomplishment unappreciated by the peasants, who vanished at the first sight of us. We located the headman. Rumors had been circulating that when Ram Sewak and I came we would grab the men and force them into vasectomies. I looked around in some disgust. Where were the policemen to carry out this plot?

Ram Sewak convinced the old headman that we merely wanted to talk. We looked so tired from our ride that no one could have feared we would abduct him. The old man seemed satisfied and went off into the village to round up the runaways. Ram Sewak and I collapsed on the nearest cot.

Eventually eight or nine men drifted toward us on the shady side of the lane and Ram Sewak began speaking in local dialect. We had been running our meetings as panels, each of us taking a turn at leading the discussion. But the first time I tried to present a point, everyone laughed and the headman explained that he was the only person in Kohlua Kahlan who could speak Hindustani. The men rarely met outsiders and never needed any language but their own dialect.

Kohlua Kahlan was isolated, but it nevertheless had heard most of the usual stories about family planning. Did Muslims practice it? Didn't the vasectomy have serious side effects? Ram Sewak cited Muslim villages receptive to family planning and explained how simple the operation was. But the men repeated their tales. One village, they claimed, had been struck by sickness after some men had the operation. Ram Sewak sighed. He asked if the villagers had, perhaps, offended a Brahmin? I could hardly believe what I was hearing. Ram Sewak claimed to be an atheist. But his maneuver succeeded. The villagers soon forgot the connection between the operation and the sickness and spent half an hour recounting various stories of the curses of Brahmins and disputing which one was closest to the present instance. I marveled again at Ram Sewak's talent for manipulating traditional and modern ideas and recalled that his caste, the Bhoomiars, had used political pressure to get themselves listed on the last census as "Brahmins," a title to which they were not traditionally entitled and which other Brahmins refused to recognize. But there it was, in black and white in the census.

Even Ram Sewak's mingling of the new and the old could not, in one meeting, bring this obstinate group of men around.

With luck, stamina, and careful pathfinding, we might come to Kohlua Kahlan three or four times in the year, meet with different groups of men each time, and deliver the same message: "You can decide how many children you want, how many sons will be needed to bring in future harvests, how many daughters you will be able to marry off in twenty years." But could the bits and pieces that Ram Sewak slipped into the traditions in Kohlua Kahlan survive? When one disastrous drought is forgotten another arrives to remind the headman that the rains depend on God and that man's fate drifts with the weather. The theme of helplessness is perpetuated. What daily reminder would preserve the memory of the day the sahibs came and talked about loops and condoms and operations?

On our way to meetings like this, or during the evenings while he drank tea in our dining room with Judy and me, Ram Sewak spoke of his past and of his ideas for the future. His home was near the Ganges in Patna District, in a region of good irrigation and agricultural prosperity. The Bhoomiars had thrust themselves upward in the social structure by industry and energy. Ram Sewak had four brothers who cultivated his share of the family rice lands for him. He was thirty-nine or forty—no one knew exactly. He had been married nineteen years, but his first child, a daughter, had only been born the past hot season.

He had originally entered training as a male nurse, but just as he completed it the Health Ministry abolished the position. So he qualified as an auxiliary health worker and had been working in subcenters like Champadih for nineteen years when the order came assigning him as Extension Educator for Barhi Block.

The loss of his private practice had hurt; he would not remain in family planning for long. "If they try to keep me here, I will resign. What is the good of my training in health if I can't use it? But if I resign, I will have to go back to my family."

"I tell my brothers, 'How can you live this way?' They get up in the morning, they go out and push the button to start the irrigation pumps . . . ping . . . they go lie on the veranda and drink tea, then in the evening they get up and turn off the pump . . . ping. Two *pings* is all the work they ever do. I can't stand that. If I go back I will supervise the agriculture myself. I have to work."

He had wanted to be a male nurse, the post was abolished, so he entered another training program. Trained, prosperous, and respected in Champadih, he was sentenced to loss of income, dignity, and freedom in the Siberia of the family planning program. Bureaucracy permitted him to delay, so he generally delayed. But unlike Mandel, he did not regard his work as onerous; and unlike Judy and me, he really felt that the Health Ministry, despite all its arbitrariness, was helping people.

Judy and I were glad to have him come to our house as often as possible. He admired the house and treated it as part of us, as something that could tell him more about the way we lived. Most people saw it as a tourist attraction; but then, most people saw Judy and me as tourists.

Although the bedroom and the dining room were side by side at the front of the house, with doors opening onto the porch, we had begun to think of them as back room and front room. We used the door which led into the dining room and entered the bedroom only from the inside, from the courtyard. When I finally put up screening, I sealed off the outside door to the bedroom.

Each room came to represent one of the two worlds that Judy and I were trying to unite. The bedroom served as our private place. Into its shelves, trunks, and wardrobe we tucked all those things we kept from America and did not wish to entrust to Barhi—old friendships folded up in letters, recipes in Judy's cookbook for American food, the outside world blazoned on a Pan-Am travel calendar, and our marriage, symbolized by the fights and reconciliations reserved for that room.

Constructed of brick, mud, and whitewash, the room was Bihari in its surfaces. But its geometry, the way we hung curtains to hide the cluttered shelves, our attempts to match the bedspread and the curtains, the arrangement of furniture established that this was an American room. It was the highpoint of the guided tour we gave old widows, who would come again in a few months with relatives from other towns to show them how the sahibs live.

The dining room became our public room, our Indian room, used for meals or for drinking tea, for entertaining Indian friends, for arranging schedules with Ram Sewak, Mrs. Srivastava, or other members of the staff. Mostly it was a room for rituals. There we ate Indian food at Indian mealtimes—seven A.M., one-thirty, eight P.M. We drank endless cups of tea with visitors who segregated themselves by sex and social standing in the way of Barhi.

Jagdish considered the dining room his, to enter, to clean, to rearrange, just as any servant in any house in Barhi might have. But he always knocked before coming into the bedroom. During the Family Planning Fortnight, Ram Sewak established the custom of arriving at eight, bellowing for me to get ready, then sitting at the dining room table waiting for me to get into some clothes so that I could join him for a cup of tea.

When Westerners arrived—hitchhikers passing through on the Grand Trunk Road, or Peace Corps staff—we would abandon the dining room table after lunch, retreat to the American room, and sprawl over the bed to exchange stories of India or of home.

This segregation had never been formalized. We often took Indians to the bedroom, but always for some specific purpose: to show the mukhia's daughter a new shawl of Judy's, for Judy to explain to one of her friends about Tampax, for me to loan a friend fifty rupees. We played cards with Westerners in the bedroom, and with Indians in the dining room. We tended, even between ourselves, to speak Hindi in the dining room and English in the bedroom. I don't think Ram Sewak ever noticed the distinction. There always seemed some good reason for sitting in one room or the other, but we had unconsciously managed to keep the separate character of each room. The division served some emotional need, and I was beginning to recognize that under the stresses of life in Barhi, my emotional needs were as real as Barhi's.

The strains of having a master-servant relationship continued to result in the skirmishes with Jagdish. Judy and I controlled the purse, the combination locks, and our tempers. Jagdish knew that we had hired him to make life easier for ourselves and therefore had limited energy for the battle. Did he likewise know that we did not believe in our side? He worked in the house, cooked food in our kitchen, and was affected by whatever decisions we made. But he was not a member of our family and did not share in our decisions. It was closeness without intimacy, and Judy and I, who had grown up in small families, were not used to it.

Others in Barhi found the master-servant relationship a natural extension of their joint families. Servants were one rung lower in the family hierarchy than the most junior family members but were sheltered under the same emotional and financial umbrella. But the relationship, which protected the servant from hunger, denied him dignity. Jagdish winced whenever Mr. Kumar or B. P. Katriar came to visit and called him to bring them a chair or a glass of water or the salt. They assured us that this was the only way to live with servants.

Jagdish's own father, a cook, stood at the end of this line of thought. He was not old, but his life as a servant had aged him. He bore with him a dependency that ought to come only when the body cannot carry out the will of the mind; in this case the mind had abdicated control. He drank. I always tried to avoid him because he greeted me by hurling his hands together in a grotesque caricature of the namaste, raising them as if to drive his body into servility. He would pile the Urdu term for "excellency" on top of the Hindi: "Pranam, Huzoor!"

We did not want any part of this master-servant relationship, but we could only avoid it by an uncomfortable formality that probably left Jagdish quite unsure how he fitted into our household. Ram Sewak treated Jagdish comfortably as another member of the household, an equal of Judy and me, almost a translator of our strange way of life. When Ram Sewak came to tea he to would summon Jagdish from the kitchen to ask for sugar or milk for the tea. He used the familiar form of address, but Jagdish did not mind. The resentment he felt when other Indians treated him casually was absent.

In Ram Sewak Jagdish found a friend who cared about food. Ram Sewak's wife was a peasant woman who spoke only dialect and prepared good but simple village food. She suited Ram Sewak's way of living in everything but diet, for he was an adventurous eater. Alone of our friends in Barhi he was eager to try, and to like, new foods. And in the Indian and Western dishes which Jagdish prepared for us, Ram Sewak found the variety he craved. Even peculiarly American tastes appealed to him. He loved peanut butter and asked Jagdish for his favorite peanut butter muffins whenever he came to tea.

That friendship meant that Jagdish had someone else to talk to when we were gone, someone who had some idea of what life with the Popes was like. Ram Sewak soon began asking Jagdish to cook for him on the days when Judy and I were shopping in

Hazaribagh.

But I noted a difference between the two which showed in their banter. Jagdish retained his boyishness, the ability to ask "Why?" He had grown up as Harijan, son of an alcoholic father, without resigning himself to all that his birth and family implied. Standing in our doorway while Judy, Ram Sewak, and I praised his curries, he would grin. Ram Sewak, an inveterate gossip, would begin the story of the troubles of some family. "Very sad situation. Her father-in-law steals from the house, he demands expensive suits from the husband if he wants his wife to come back after a visit, and the poor husband gives in."

Jagdish would frown, an intense look on his face, and he would stop Ram Sewak. "But that isn't right. Why does he do that? A father-in-law should help his son-in-law take care of the woman."

Ram Sewak would nod his head and agree. His willingness to help the family if he could was as genuine as Jagdish's. But, as he often replied, "It's that way." Which, I noted, Jagdish did not accept. I was not sure which was odder—Ram Sewak's compassionate helpfulness without any expectation that it would change anything, or Jagdish's persistent and innocent question "Why?" in an environment that never answered him.

9.

By the end of the fortnight Dr. Agarwal was ready to test whether the daily round of meetings and propaganda had paid off. He arranged to visit several of the villages to perform vasectomy operations on the spot. Village headmen had promised that some men would be ready. But Dr. Agarwal also scheduled these "camps" to coincide with land surveys being conducted by the Development Officer. "Mr. Kumar can help us a great deal," he told me. I wondered how. Mr. Kumar was a strong supporter of family planning but completely detached from the villages and the peasants.

The land survey was held in the village school. Ram Sewak would arrive in the morning. Mr. Kumar would be seated at a desk, with the headmen around him on the floor. One by one the peasants would come forward to present their claims to land which they had reclaimed from the scrub forest. The huge deeds they brandished as evidence of their old holdings were printed with the seal of the British Raj. Ram Sewak whispered to me that the last land review in Bihar had taken place before World War II, and that records had become hopelessly scrambled. When a dispute arose, Mr. Kumar and the village leaders would get in the jeep and drive out to inspect the land. I was not used to government officials looking at anything as real as land.

Each dispute seemed to boil down to one man's word against another's. Yet even where there was no dispute Mr. Kumar signed no new deeds. When the last case had been reviewed, I waited for Mr. Kumar to begin signing. He sat there, waiting. For what, I did not know. Just then Dr. Agarwal drove up in the jeep. He got out, Mr. Kumar greeted him, and they both went to talk to the headmen. The pile of pending deeds was gone through again. Occasionally the headmen would nod. Dr. Agarwal would ask a question or two, and that deed would be laid aside. Finally about ten deeds had been put aside. Mr. Kumar signed the rest.

Then he called over the ten men whose claims were pending, and he and the doctor talked to them about the vasectomy. I was uneasy. The headmen had *said* that ten men were willing to have the operation, and I was quite sure that Mr. Kumar would actually sign the deeds even if one of them refused. But I was not sure that the peasants realized this.

As the doctor and Mr. Kumar sat there, in their Western clothes, pressuring small landowners whose cotton garments did not conceal their spindly legs, my old anger arose at the forms Western culture had taken in India. This was coercion—coercion out of good motives. The men had been carefully screened, all had six or seven children, none could feed them properly with their present landholdings. But the government claimed that people were supposed to learn to decide these things for themselves. If coercion was going to be applied, it should have been applied equally against everyone. This was bullying.

And I was bothered because I knew that B. P. Katriar used this kind of pressure every day, without offending me nearly as much, simply because both he and the peasant wore cotton dhotis and Dr. Agarwal wore a dacron suit. I got up and left.

Ram Sewak was outside talking to the clerk who had set up a table for the records. The discussion inside was over and five or six of the men waited in line. I was relieved to see that two of the men walked in the other direction, carrying their deeds with them.

The clerk began taking the seven fingerprints required of each patient. Ram Sewak and I, in a routine we had developed, walked around to the back of the building, where a small window opened on to the schoolroom where Dr. Agarwal was scrubbing up to prepare for the operations. When the first patient came in, the men waiting in line began to sneak back one by one. They would run up to the window to peek; then, noticing Ram Sewak and me, would walk off into the fields as if they had to urinate. We waited until we knew that the patient inside was far enough along in the operation not to notice a head or two at the window. Then we casually walked back to the front of the school and looked off into the distance. The line of men melted away. Seen through the window, the operation was nothing at all, and we wanted the men to know this. But we didn't want the patient's privacy violated.

No one complained and everyone got to see.

Meanwhile, Judy and Dr. Malik had plunged ahead with their work among the women. The perpetual shortage of gas for the jeep was solved by an order from Dr. Gope in Hazaribagh that Dr. Malik would do loop insertions in a number of nearby blocks. This meant that he *had* to provide money for gasoline. Dr. Malik was mobile.

The first clinic had been scheduled in Dhanwar Block, about thirty miles from Barhi. Once again the jeep was loaded to the roof, but Judy reported that the atmosphere was quite different from the days when ten or twelve of us accompanied Dr. Agarwal. Dr. Malik's sunny personality turned the whole day into what Indians call a "tamasha" (a "spectacle"). Everyone laughed at jammed fingers, at the lurching sterilizer that threatened to fly out the rear at every corner, at near collisions with goats. There was none of the sense of authority that never left Dr. Agarwal, and Judy did not have to choose between Dr. Malik and the staff.

Of course, there were no cases when they got to Dhanwar. The doctor there insisted that he had not been informed. But he promised that there would be cases at one of his subcenters. Dr. Malik sent the jeep to find out. The subcenter was supposed to be seven miles away, but the jeep did not return for two hours. Girja, who was driving, reported no cases. The subcenter staff claimed that the women would be found at the marketplace, another five miles in the direction of Barhi. The bazaar had been searched, to no avail.

Everyone clambered over the sterilizer and back into the jeep. On the drive back to Barhi they came to the market town where Girja had hunted. Dr. Malik asked Girja to stop. She was determined to convince some women to take a loop.

When Judy told me this I shook my head. Dr. Malik might be skillful at maintaining morale in a crowded jeep, but she was an innocent about village women. A total stranger was not going to convince them to take time off from a busy market day to have a strange medical device stuck inside them to prevent the conception of babies at some future date.

Dr. Malik found some women, set them down and started gossiping. Judy reported that she spoke the village dialect perfectly. She talked about their problems as women. "Look at our lot. We have to cook the meals, care for the children, keep the house, while our husbands go out every night and drink tea with their friends. And when the next child comes, when we have given birth at 3 A.M., what do we get? Rest? Oh, no! At 6 A.M. the men want us to get up and make their breakfast!"

I was beginning to think that Dr. Malik could be a very effective propagandist. In four or five visits she probably would convince some women, especially if she also provided some basic medical care.

"Then," Judy went on, "she brought out the loop kit."

I shuddered. The loop kit was a gaudy, audio-visual device which we had all been given in training. It was designed to demonstrate the reproductive anatomy of a woman and the manner in which the loop was inserted. In addition to a cut-away 3-D model of the reproductive organs, the kit included an inserter, a loop, and a hollow plastic uterus. The demonstrator could open the loop kit's first panel, show in graphic pink and red detail the external genitalia, place the inserter in the plastic vagina, push in the loop, and open the second panel to show the loop nestled inside the clear plastic uterus.

It had been made clear to us in training that we could use this model to train the staff, who were used to these ideas, but that it would be more than squeamish villagers could take.

Apparently they had loved it. One minute they had been sitting around, sometimes listening, sometimes gossiping. The next minute they had knotted up in a huddle and fallen absolutely silent.

I asked Judy how Dr. Malik had reacted when she failed to get any cases. Judy laughed. "But she didn't fail. Seven women had the loop inserted."

This news forced me to reshape my image of Barhi. Maybe miracles *were* possible.

Dr. Malik remained indifferent to paper, to orders, and to Dr. Gope. He had intended the money he gave for petrol for use only outside the block. But as she brightly pointed out, even he could not object if on her way outside the block she stopped off to do additional work at Champadih or Kariatpur, both of which were on main roads.

A number of women near Barhi had wanted the loop, and Judy came back happy from the first day of insertions. Dr. Malik had taken Judy's suggestion of a lecture to the women before the insertion on all the medical aspects of the loop, its possible side effects, their treatment. She had used the loop kit, again with success. She continued her careful sterile procedures.

Then a small cloud gathered inside my head. I asked Judy who had brought the women for the insertion. She told me that it was the village chamain, or midwife, the same one who had brought cases to Dr. Narayin when we had first come to Barhi. I reminded her of the fistful of bloody loops found behind the hospital.

"How many of those loops do you think are in place to-night?" I asked her.

"One?" she ventured.

I held up my fingers, looped in a circle.

Nevertheless, Ram Sewak and Dr. Malik had shaken my passivism. I decided that the problem of identifying repeaters had a solution.

In a joking mood, one of the Peace Corps staff had once suggested tatooing the women. Well . . . the women in the Barhi area sported long lines of blue tatooing on their necks, their wrists, and around their ankles. Perhaps some sort of additional mark could be slipped in, say at the wrist, where no one would notice it unless he was looking. We could instruct the clerk to look before letting women sign up for the loop. It shouldn't be difficult. I still had a small black mark on my knee where I drove a pencil under the skin in seventh grade.

My system would have to be foolproof. I would have to experiment on myself. I tried using India ink and a sterilized sewing needle. Deep pricks did not work; blood welled out and washed out the cuts. So I tried a shallow, glancing stroke with the needle, which left a little black hentrack under the skin. It was clear enough, but would it last? We tried it out one day at the hospital. (Dr. Agarwal approved the idea. Apparently the bureaucracy had no regulations against tatooing in the family planning program.) The women wailed at the pricks; but then they wailed before the pricks. In four or five days my little black marks faded.

I couldn't figure out how the village women produced the long blue tatoos. I was sure it hurt. I wanted something relatively painless. So I broke out the disposable syringes Judy and I had with us for travel. Swabbing the inside of my forearm with alcohol, I loaded the syringe with India ink, pricked the skin, and injected a small quantity. Instead of the neat black dot I had expected, the ink ran under my skin in a long splotch. It hurt. I was amazed at how much it hurt. Still, with refinements I might be able to adapt it. Perhaps this would be my major contribution to family planning.

In three days my arm began to swell; pain ran up and down the large knot that was forming. The blue stain had spread, but a small black dot did remain. So far there were none of the red streaks that would mean serious blood poisoning.

I felt justly punished. What had happened to my sense of proportion? How had I managed in a little over nine months to forget that I was supposed to be helping the women, not trying to prevent them from practicing petty fraud on a government that certainly practiced grand larceny on them? The swelling and pain disappeared, leaving a permanent blue splotch, a most unheroic wound, and a chastened Volunteer.

Dr. Malik solved the problem of repeaters by the simple expedient of remembering their faces. Apparently no one else had ever bothered to try, and I had been convinced that it was impossible. Numbers had been getting to me again, numbers and the sameness that poverty imposed on the women.

Within two weeks Dr. Malik could identify all her repeaters, and when they showed up again she gestured and threatened them with the police and other terrors if they kept coming. She grinned with satisfaction as a woman scuttled away, holding her ragged sari in front of her. "She's poor, but I can't spend my time inserting a loop in her twice a day. Anyway, she'll tear her uterus apart that way. Who's next?"

10. October and November were coming, the best months in the calendar. The paddy was ripening, and after the near drought of August the peasants were happy at the prospect of a fair crop. We too were happy. In two months Judy and I had discovered co-workers who went beyond our expectations. If Ram Sewak could conduct meetings as skillfully as he did, if Dr. Malik could walk into a strange market and convince seven women to accept the loop, then something was possible.

But, the fortnight had worn everyone down. We had been working about six hours a day, and six hours in Barhi was at least twice as much as anyone had worked before the fortnight. October would be mostly lost anyway, for the peasants would be in the paddies or celebrating Durga Puja and Diwali, the two greatest holidays of the Hindu calendar. The members of the medical staff would scatter to their home villages. So Judy and I took off for a tour of southern and western India.

The longer we stayed in India, the more questions we learned to ask. But in every situation there seemed to be one crucial one we overlooked. Thus, on this tour, when we were about to leave the ancient Portuguese city of Cochin, we made certain that the buses near our hotel stopped at the airport, and that they left every fifteen minutes. We timed the trip to the airport—fifteen minutes. We called the airline and asked how early we had to arrive for our flight. We added an extra twenty minutes for accidents, flat tires, or heavy traffic.

Late in the afternoon we hauled our luggage out to the stand at the harborside and waited while bus after bus came, loaded up, and left. Each time the conductor said, "No Sahib. This bus doesn't pass the airport." Finally I approached the dispatcher, the man who had told us that a bus came every fifteen minutes.

"When will there be an airport bus?"

He spat out a mouthful of betel juice and pointed to a bus which had just pulled in. "That one." I turned to go. "But it's rush hour."

"I'm used to crowds," I told him. "We'll jam in."

"No, Sahib. He won't take your luggage. It will slow him down."

"Have all these buses been going to the airport?"

"Yes. You'll have to take a taxi."

Taxis didn't come to this part of old Cochin. I ran over to Judy in a panic. "Hurry up. Get on this bus. They don't want to take us."

"Why not?"

"It's rush hour, and they don't want to wait while we unload our bags. Come on!"

We picked up our bags and waited in line. No one in Bihar waited in line, so just being in queue was a relief. When I got to the steps the conductor hailed me. "Oh, Sahib, where are you going?"

"Airport, Conductor Sahib."

"Next bus, Sahib."

He tried to stand in my way. "Dispatcher said *this* bus," I told him. He started to glance over at the dispatcher, and I took the chance to slip past him and pile my bag on the top of the steps. I reached around the still protesting conductor and pulled Judy aboard. The conductor nearly fell off the step.

Each time we outwitted the system it was a small triumph. To an Indian, outwitting the system is a daily necessity; systems do not work, and as far the Indian can tell, they cannot work. As we rode to the airport I thought about this difference. My own experience told me that systems can work; one need only insist that they *do* work. I put the thought away. The South was beautiful, there were sights and experiences to be savored.

When we got back to Barhi, the women were stripping and replacing the red tile roofs, replastering walls eroded by the rains with a mixture of clay and cow dung, scrubbing window frames and doors, and covering outside walls with a thin cow dung paint applied in swirls with their palms. The rice was bent over, the tips turning yellow as the grain ripened. The pale new leaves of the sisum, which had come with the first force of the monsoon, had darkened until they almost matched the holly glisten of the mango. Tomatoes and peas were heaped on the burlap sacks of the market women.

Durga Puja had passed, but it was still two days until Diwali. The children next door came to show us their new white outfits, and two of the mukhia's laborers began to whitewash the front porch of our house. The fantastic cloud formations of the monsoon were gone. Long purple bands ran around the horizon at sunset, and at night the stars sparkled. The same wind was blowing, the wind that fought Ram Sewak and me on the way to Kohlua Kahlan, but since I had nowhere to go I could relax and enjoy the patterns it made in the ricefields.

Jagdish whistled as he ground up the spices, the turmeric, onion, garlic, clove, and pepper for the chicken we would have for dinner. We regretted that Ram Sewak had gone home to Patna District for the week, especially when Jagdish asked if he could make peanut butter muffins.

Judy visited the mukhia's house during the day, sitting in the dark kitchen while Shobha cooked. I took the bus to Hazaribagh to bring back clay lamps for the festival. The hardy perennial marigolds that had pushed up everywhere in the monsoon were in full blossom and grew faster than the children next door could pluck them to make prayer garlands.

The day of Diwali was sunny. Jagdish had carefully instructed me on which type of oil to obtain for the lamps and in Hazaribagh I had bought fireworks. After breakfast we dressed up the compound. Hundreds of small clay lamps fitted with string wicks had to be placed. We put them at eight-inch intervals along the flat ridges of the compound wall, on window ledges, around the brick facing of the well, on top of the rafter over our door, and finally along the edge of the path which Arun and Bige, Prasad Babu's eldest sons, had laid out with brick to discourage people from trampling their garden. At noon Anuj Katriar came by and invited us to lunch with the mukhia. In Bangalore Judy had bought a flaming striped sari of orange, purple, and reds, which the shop girl had assured her was "the latest fashion." If it was the latest fashion, Barhi had yet to encounter it.

On the way to the Katriars' we passed workmen on ladders who were lining each cove and roof line of the cold storage plant with larger, closed lamps that dwarfed our own. Shobha greeted us. The furniture had been removed, and soon Mr. Kumar, Madan Babu, the local contractor, Dr. Agarwal, and the rest of the town elite were seated beside us along the bedroom wall.

Anuj brought an armful of broad banana leaves. Shobha followed with crude clay bowls. Then several cooks loaded the leaf plates and the bowls with meat and fish curry, tomato chutney, peas pullao, lentil soup, and a thick pile of chappatis. The food, as always, was delicious, and no one talked, except to praise it and nod when the cook made the rounds again, doling out the pullao from a huge pail. Gorged, content, we moved out to the porch and rinsed our hands. Behind us the servants picked up the leaves and clay pots, piled them in a basket and took them to the compost heap to rot.

We slept during the afternoon, and as dark came Jagdish and I carefully filled each of the small clay lamps with peanut oil, replacing a few wicks that had blown off. Everyone was waiting for a signal that it was time to light the lamps and shoot off the fireworks. Behind us, a few lights appeared through the mango trees. Prasad Babu and his family were in the yard with us. Arun and Bige were dancing about. "Is it time, Papa, is it time?" The girls stayed next to Judy, their eyes on the bags of sparklers and fireworks. They weren't going to miss anything. Judy and I shared their excitement. Prasad Babu, ostentatiously consulting his watch to make very clear that he was no illiterate peasant dependent on the sky to tell time, announced that it was dark enough. Instantly the girls and boys surrounded the cot, holding out their hands for candles.

I kept one for myself to light the highest rows on the roof, and the children and I made our way around the compound. We had to shield the candles from the breeze, but the lamps, once lit, flared up brightly in the dark. The well rim became a flickering ring; the heavy oil smoke rose above it, reflecting the glow of the lamps. I could see the workmen on their ladders moving down the long rows of lamps on the cold storage plant. The line of light was halfway up the slope of the roof, and the doorways and alcoves were etched in a soft yellow glow. I felt, looking around at the outlines of cow sheds, garden fences, rooftops, and temples, that it was a new creation, that the gods had truly begun their work with "Let there be light." The cold storage plant was climbing into the sky; our house and the compound were alive with light. The roof tiles sloped back into the shadow above the top row of lamps; the house had been given a low, sleek profile. Above it the mango leaves seemed cut out of the starry sky. Judy, Prasad Babu, and his wife sat on a cot, surrounded by hissing lamps which the smallest boy had placed so that he too could have something to light.

So far this new world was devoid of color. It was time to embroider the scene with fireworks. Bige had dug a shallow hole for the small rockets, candles, fountains and flares. Everyone stood back, and as I planted the rockets the children stared straight up at the sky, waiting for the burst above their heads. Rockets had been forbidden my childhood; I was unsure about the safety of these. So I was just as nervous as the children as I lit the first. It swished up about fifty feet and broke out in a brilliant blue ball. I fired off the rest; each was followed by exclamations from the children as they let out deep breaths, and the youngest commented wonderingly after they were finished, "Are' Baap!" ("Look, Father!") We all laughed.

I gave Arun the candle so that he could touch off the fuses of the fountains and flares. Around us now other rockets were going off over other backyards. The yellow and red puddles of light from the torches lured the children from around the cot, and they stood there, holding hands and silently watching the flares. By now our crude lamps were exhausting their supply of oil. The demise of each was marked by a burst of oily smoke. The ring around the well had grown ragged, but above us the steep gable of the cold storage plant still stood, its line of lights dominating everything.

All of Barhi was a fairyland. The shape of the houses, the chalky surface of the whitewash, the bending mangoes, the low porches, the niches and alcoves, all seemed designed for this one night. The smoke diffused the light, so that except for the cold storage plant in its pride, each building was wrapped in a halo. So many lamps had been hung from porches and along roofs and in the corners of windows that the hissing of the oil could be heard everywhere.

By day the scene was chaos: cow bells, noisy brakes, jackals, chattering crowds, transistor radios with their film songs, incense, rotting vegetables and cow dung, dust and bus exhaust, gaudy store signs, faded saris, neon lights; all these clashed and exhausted the senses. Now the even light, the smell of oil, and the hissing of a thousand lamps had woven the disparate elements into a magic web.

11. Ram Sewak returned after Diwali. We were both in a mood to start something different, something that would make the program in Barhi look vigorous enough so that the rest of the family planning staff would begin to develop an interest. Dr. Das, the touring family planning doctor from the district office in Hazaribagh, was fond of suggesting that the key to changing village attitudes was to get the lowly condom available everywhere in the villages. He claimed this would give the villager a simple, one-time way of getting in the habit of "planning." He was convinced of it.

"No one used to drink tea," he said. "During the war, with exports blocked, the Tea Board went into every village. Their promoters set up small stoves and brewed tea right in the middle of the market. They gave away free samples, at first using mostly milk and sugar, gradually increasing the strength of the tea. Then they began to sell it, and today the villager thinks he would die if a day passed without a cup."

The same thing could be done for the condom. "It doesn't matter if we give them to a man and he throws them away; someone else will pick them up. Things always get picked up in this country."

And from higher up, from Patna, orders kept piling up on Dr. Agarwal's desk to increase condom use. The clerk's file on "contraceptive distribution" bulged with memoranda until the little white tape that held them together would no longer reach around.

Ram Sewak and I convinced Dr. Agarwal to take the plunge.

We would give free condoms for distribution to every school-teacher who wanted a supply. The teachers, who came in every month to get their paychecks, were under the supervision of Mr. Kumar. Mr. Kumar was friendly, and hung around with the young men most likely to use the condom, the most educated and outward-looking peasants or salaried workers.

The idea seemed free of the pitfalls that dogged Ram Sewak and me in our attempts to work within the Health Ministry. We would control the recordkeeping. Instead of trying to use resistant people like Mandel to create a communications channel, we would take advantage of an existing social network.

Ram Sewak and I asked Mrs. Srivastava for the key to her office and the cabinet in which she stored the contraceptives. "Only one key," she said, unhooking it from the end of her sari. "I have only one lock, so when I leave the room I take it off the closet and put it on the door. Then when I open the office I lock up the closet."

"But," I protested, "what's the point of locking the closet when you're there in the office? How do you get at the supplies to give them out?"

"Oh, I never need to get at them," she replied. "No one wants those things anyway."

Ram Sewak and I got out the condoms and counted. We had six hundred. I estimated that each customer would need about 8 in an average month. Ram Sewak, with his theories about libido and health, felt this was excessive. One or two ought to do. But I pointed out to him that if abstinence, or at least continence, meant good health, and indulgence bad, then the villagers in Barhi must be indulging. We asked Dr. Agarwal.

"Why, give the man as many as he wants . . . it will vary from individual to individual. Some men, even using the condom regularly, will need one or two a month, while some . . ." here he paused, searching for the outermost plausible figure, "why some men might need as many as . . . ten!"

Ram Sewak didn't believe it but agreed to use six as an average. This meant that we could supply one hundred men in the first month. We picked twenty-five teachers from among those we had met during the fortnight. They all agreed to try to find four friends who would use the condoms. We gave each of them an unlined register in which to keep records. A number of other teachers wanted condoms, either for their own use or for friends. We promised them a supply when they came in to get their paychecks.

The next month Ram Sewak and I were able to supply twenty-five teachers and distribute over twelve hundred condoms. Everyone said that there was a large demand and asked for an even larger supply for the following month. Dr. Agarwal insisted that some records be kept so that we would know where we stood; Ram Sewak and I asked each teacher how many men were using the condoms. Forty-five teachers were using the condoms themselves.

We emphasized the condom in our meetings in the villages. We began, as Dr. Das suggested, to hand them to everyone, at least one or two samples. In January we gave out over two thousand. It was a good omen for Judy's and my first anniversary in Barhi. At this rate, we would achieve the government's three-year target by the end of six months! I prepared elaborate charts for the next visit by the Civil Surgeon. I wanted to prove to Dr. Gope that Barhi had a better record than the All-India average, and that we had ten-fold the results of the rest of the state of Bihar. I thought it was conceivable that he might then give Dr. Agarwal a little support.

I even began proseletyzing the condom outside of Barhi Block. On trips to Hazaribagh to pick up fresh supplies I usually had to wait for the bus to Barhi. I gathered a crowd, took out one of the little blue packets, and pointed to the red triangle printed on it. I explained that this triangle stood for family planning, for the idea that having children was something you could decide. Stealing shamelessly from Ram Sewak, I told them that if there was no seed in the field there would be no crop. The condom was a little rubber bag to hold all the seed. I gave each man one or two and said they could get more at any health center. In February we passed out three thousand condoms.

In two weeks Barhi would celebrate Holi, the ancient fertility festival of India, the spring Saturnalia. On Holi, people in the street threw colored water on each other; little else remained to mark its bacchanalian character. But people began to come up to me in the market and ask for a special supply of condoms, "just for Holi." Some of the spirit survived, at least in private. The schoolteachers all wanted extra supplies for the month. One,

Chaudrikhar Mahato, insisted that he needed 144 condoms, a whole carton. I asked if he had brought his register listing how many men were using the condoms. He had forgotten it. So had everyone else. I didn't have enough condoms, so I told him he could not have that many until he brought in his register. I was not bothered by the lack of registers; the increase in demand was quite intoxicating. Something was happening.

Meanwhile, Dr. Malik had finished inserting the loops in Barhi itself. After she started turning away the repeaters, very few women came. There was still too much fear of the side effects.

But Dr. Malik was all set to work the rest of the block systematically. The jeep, quixotically, was in running order, though there was no money to buy gasoline. Dr. Malik went to Dr. Gope, who fussed and mumbled but offered no help. Dr. Malik wrote letters to the ministry in Patna. No reply. It was up to Judy and me to go to Patna. Perhaps the sahibs could con the bureaucracy out of some gasoline money.

The offices of the ministry were located in the New Secretariat, which was no longer new. We entered the concrete building by a set of dark stairs guarded by a sentry. Corridors ran around four sides of a dingy courtyard. The cement floor of the court had been dyed red by the betel stains of men spitting from the upper floors, and every few minutes a clerk would lean over the rail and add a fresh splotch. The paint had peeled off the walls of the courtyard and lay, unswept, in piles in the drain.

We picked our way around great wooden cupboards, benches, offices set up in halls. Across from every door was a chair for the peon who guarded access and a bench for those who waited to enter. Everything moved in slow motion. Even the typewriters clacked slowly and deliberately.

Over each curtained doorway hung a wooden sign with engraved Hindi and English titles. We finally located the one that said "Additional Director of Health Service for Family Planning—Dr. Brij Bansi Prasad." A peon outside the office rested his head on his chest, his hat about to fall off. I spoke to him: "Is the Sahib in?"

"No, Sahib. He's in a meeting." He put his head down again. The secretariat had not been set up to deal with dusty villages. It handled the reports and files sent in each month from the blocks, the ruled and inked registers listing couples contacted, motivated, postnatal visits, number of days on tour, number of night halts.

Every month, orders issued from the typewriters of the secretariat that these reports should be filed, and every month the fabricated reports generated demands for more records.

The employees on the wooden benches, waiting their turn to see an assistant director about a transfer, were not there to do business with the secretariat. It was the files they carried, the memoranda from the block doctor, the appealing note from the man himself beginning "Most honored and revered sir" that the secretariat would judge. Each man was merely a messenger carrying a file. The clerks at their desks used their energy to protect themselves and their superiors from Bihar.

As I waited for the peon to look up again, dhoti-clad men ambled back and forth, carrying mud-red files labeled "midwife training" or "intensive programs." The files were bound with white tape, to counter the public impression that the ministry was insufficiently responsive because of "red tape."

Finally the peon looked up. "Do you mind if we sit down and wait for the Sahib?" I asked.

"Sit inside. He'll be back."

We pushed aside the curtain. Each wall was lined with shelves of folders and registers. On the desk, ten or so letters had been inserted under the corners of the green blotter. A black telephone rang. I looked at the curtain expecting the peon to rush in, hold the receiver at a respectful arm's length, and bellow, "Yes, who is it?" But no peon came. I watched the phone for a few minutes until it quit ringing. The isolation of Brij Bansi Prasad from the dirty lane that ran past our compound and from the children who played in that lane was total.

Or, I thought, would be, unless Judy and I managed somehow to bring something of the village into this office. At least we had come ourselves, bearing no paper. Dr. Prasad would have to deal with us. But perhaps the fact that we were using our prestige as foreigners undid the effect of this? I think that Dr. Prasad himself wondered how to reconcile our being Americans, well paid, well educated, and willing to *use* those advantages, with the fact that we kept talking to him about the real life of the villages, which he would rather have ignored.

Dr. Prasad was not to blame for this. He had not asked for

the Volunteers, at least not the ones he got. He had been offered the services, free, of a number of eager young sahibs trained in extension education techniques. Dr. Prasad, Dr. Gope, and the others had thought we would see that the lower-level staff worked. They had expected overseers who would employ American enthusiasm and drive. No more.

Instead, we came to their offices in Hazaribagh or Patna, pounded their desks, advised our block doctors to ignore the latest circular, scolded clerks, and encouraged the staff not to keep their records. Instead of telling Mrs. Srivastava to walk five miles every day, Judy and I tried to get the government to release her travel allowance so she could take the bus. Instead of impressing upon Ram Sewak the need to fulfill his quota, I joined him in mocking the silly piece of paper.

And now, as Dr. Prasad learned when he came in, rather than setting an example for Dr. Malik so that she would spend her own money for gas, we had come to Patna to extract money from the state treasury.

Although he may have been thoroughly tired of us and our nagging, Dr. Prasad was polite, genial, cooperative. He promised to write an order releasing some special petrol funds for the use of Barhi Block. This was quite a victory. Judy was glad to be able to take good news back to Dr. Malik, I was looking forward to rejoining Ram Sewak. We would use the jeep to get to some of the more distant villages, saving long hours on the cycles. Maybe, if Mandel knew that the jeep might come by any day to check up on him, he would at least go out and distribute some condoms. As the bus pulled into Barhi I felt rewarded. I hadn't much liked Patna or the secretariat, and Barhi was home. That night Jagdish's fish curry tasted especially good.

12. Before we could shift the family planning program into high gear, a political crisis intervened. During our stay in Bihar, the state had been ruled by a coalition government held together only by its opposition to the long-dominant Congress Party. To split this coalition the Congress Party had encouraged a group of assemblymen to defect and form a new party, the Soshit Dal. The Soshit Dal, in order to discourage defections from its own ranks, hit on the novel device of appointing every member of the party to a position in the cabinet. For a few months, Congress members of the Assembly supported this top-heavy cabinet. Then it collapsed of its own weight. New elections were called, and in February, as the date approached, the whole government began postponing decisions. No money for gas came from Patna; the schoolteachers became involved in preparations for the election; politics took precedence over family planning.

Ram Sewak and I did not mind. The election would soon be over, and I was anxious to observe an Indian vote. Both of us nurtured modest hopes that the new cabinet might push family planning.

The first sign of the impending election had been the opening in the Barhi bazaar of the Janata Party. This was the private political party of our neighbor, Raja Bahadur Kamakya Narain Sinha, the Raja of Ramgarh, the old landlord of Hazaribagh District. His former audience hall, impressive from a distance, pathetic close up, squatted about a mile from the Hazaribagh Road, in the midst of thorn and scrub. This waste had once been a dense forest, the royal hunting preserve, and its present plight symbolized the politics of the present Raja. Having deforested the district, the Raja had turned to politics to deforest the state treasury. He had been in and out of three political parties but had always returned to the Janata Party. It seemed the only comfortable political home for him, perhaps because most of its leaders were blood relatives. Hazaribagh District was represented in the national parliament in New Delhi by his wife, while he, his son, his mother, and various cousins and retainers trotted off to represent the different constituencies of Hazaribagh District in the state assembly in Patna.

Kamakya Narain Sinha's son, who had whipped B. P. Katriar in the last election, was to run again from Barhi. There was opposition. K. P. Katriar, B. P.'s cousin, ran on the Jana Sangh ticket. B. P.'s brother-in-law, a Patna lawyer, stood for the Congress. The Socialists nominated a Muslim, but he was not considered a serious candidate.

Mr. Kumar suggested that there was only one serious candidate. "The Raja has deep roots here, he spends heavily, the opposition is splintered. Most of the village leaders were his retainers before land reform, when he was landlord over most of this area. His first campaign consisted of one dinner. He invited all the village leaders to his palace and made a speech: 'We have been together many years, your families and mine. Now they say the times have changed. Now we have swaraj ("home rule") and elections, and the Congress, and Nehruji. But I say to you, all this is today, but what of tomorrow? Vote in the elections. It is the will of the government. But put your faith in the old, certain ways. Elections or no, I am your Raja, bound to protect you, and you are my people. You have eaten my salt (and he would point to the table), I have taken your word.'

"But now," said Kumar, "the Raja has faded. He has to campaign in a Russian helicopter; he gives out blankets and gifts to show that he is still the generous king. Imagine him and the Rani descending in a helicopter on some interior village without a road. People forget he is a king—they think he has become a god!"

That night at dinner I asked Jagdish about the Raja; would people in Barhi still support him?

Jagdish did not think so. In the village, where people were "simple and ignorant," the Raja might win. But he had played too many tricks on the people of Barhi. Jagdish remembered that the Raja still had not payed him for the work he did last election as a poll worker. And there had been an incident in a mine. The families of several old workers, killed in an accident, had been denied penions because the Raja forged records to show that the workers were still in their probationary period.

Jagdish planned to vote for the Congress candidate, Radha Gobind Prasad. Since he was the mukhia's brother-in-law, it was obvious that B. P. would have to campaign for him. I remembered that the mukhia had told us that he had sworn off politics. His promise, like the last legislature itself, had proved temporary.

Dr. Agarwal expressed satisfaction that there would be an election. Finally the public Works Department would have to fix the roads in the block so that the jeeps could get to the polling places on election day.

In January, when the schoolteachers came to get their pay, I listened while the election supervisor explained their duties as polling officers.

Their task was complicated. Few of the voters were literate, none carried written identification. Women came in purdah garments, so that even their neighbors could not be sure whose wife had come. The ballots, marked with pen, had to be folded in a certain way so that the mark did not smear. Poll watchers had to be satisfied that the ballot box had not been stuffed.

A local Rube Goldberg had put his mind to this last problem. The ballot box had evolved from a simple container of paper slips into a true machine, with spring operated levers, ratcheted slots, seals, and seals within seals, and a sealed canvas bag for the full box, and a sealed canvas bag to hold the seals. The very thick manual entitled *Manual for Polling Officers,* printed in English, was not available to teachers. The block had only two copies for over ninety polling stations. Each teacher serving as a polling officer attended five briefing sessions, received the same explanation at each, until he had memorized the procedures.

I had to admire the ingenuity and reliance on oral tradition. But it was another false economy. Charges of vote fraud would follow quarrels at voting stations where regulations existed only in the head of the polling officer. In a close race it could matter. But would there be any close races in Barhi? The real candidate, here as over all the district, was Bahadur Raja of Ramgarh. His name had always been victory. Could it be any different this time?

B. P. Katriar was beginning to think so. Things were looking up for the Congress Party across the state, and Radha Gobind Prasad was its outstanding candidate. The memory of twenty years of Congress rule had faded since the last election. Now people blamed the opposition for their troubles.

The Jana Sangh, too, was talking victory. They saturated the entire district with painted wall slogans: "For water in every field, work for every hand, vote Jana Sangh," or "Land, state, duty, God—vote for the Jana Sangh." "Vote for the Jana Sangh by marking the sign of the lamp." Nearly every shop in Barhi had hoisted the saffron flag with the lamp, and most of the young shopkeepers in town had taken to parading up and down in the saffron Ghandi caps with which the party challenged the white Congress caps.

Ram Sewak pointed one slogan out to me. "What a bogus party the Jana Sangh is, Pope Sahib. Look at that wall poster: 'To build an atomic and hydrogen bomb, vote the Jana Sangh.' Now who is going to build an atomic bomb? The Bihar state government? It can't even pay the streetsweepers, and the Jana Sangh knows as much about building a bomb as a streetsweeper!"

The Jana Sangh was a traditional religious party appealing to conservative sentiments. Its resurgence meant more trouble for minorities, more trouble for the family planning program, which the party systematically attacked as a Muslim plot.

We had put up seven metal family planning signboards along the roads. Four were destroyed within a week. We never caught anyone, but the bazaar knew that the Jana Sangh had organized the vandalism. A little destruction and rampaging would fire the fervor of the cadres, and lacking either the traditional appeal of the Raja or the distinguished candidate of the Congress, the Sangh in Barhi depended on fervor.

The destruction of our signs was irritating, but as the campaign quickened party workers began harassing the family planning staff. There had always been a few young men who made snide remarks at the midwives and nurses; now the insults grew more open. One of the trained midwives came to Judy in tears. The men had been warning her that the Jana Sangh would win and had added, "and when we do we'll kick family planning out, and you with it." Rumors about the side effects of the operation or the loop grew wilder; Ram Sewak and I were meeting with more stubborn resistance in our meetings.

Only the condom program ran smoothly. Many of the school-teachers supported the Jana Sangh, which must have given the scheme some protection. The paucity of stories about the condom was not unrelated to a quiet visit Ram Sewak made every month, late in the evening, to the house of K. P. Katriar. Ram Sewak reported that K. P. used a "very too much excessive" supply of condoms each month, yet his body did not seem to be degenerating.

But the attack on us did not win the party votes. To succeed, it had to convince the villagers that its traditional, patriarchal, and Hindu-dominated world could be restored. That meant real change, and Ram Sewak and I saw more and more evidence that the peasants did not any longer look to the political system for real change. They might vote for the Raja out of habit, or for Radha Gobind Prasad out of respect, but they did not expect to gain very much by it in any case.

The common question in the village was, "Sahibs, who should we vote for?" And when Ram Sewak and I asked them for *their* opinion, they would say, "Does it matter? Let God decide. It's all the same."

The Jana Sangh was flailing about, looking for an issue. Suddenly, in the middle of the campaign, the Public Works Department embarked on one of those ventures in which the Bihar bureaucracy fitfully indulged. The central government, with funds from the Ford Foundation, had launched a project to widen the national highways, including the Grand Trunk Road, to two full lanes; trucks and buses would then not have to pass each other on the dirt shoulders, which would save a number of trees and villagers from coming to harm.

There was no sign the project was getting close to Barhi, but no doubt on some contractor's schedule it should have, so the Barhi Public Works Department got ready. I came back from Hazaribagh one day to find the fish ladies evicted from their precarious perches on the roadway. Then I noticed that for about ten yards down the road all the usual knickknacks of the market had been cleared out. The fruit stalls on their wooden stilts, the vegetable vendors under their gossamer umbrellas, the benches in front of the tea stalls, the Jana Sangh banners, had all vanished. All that remained were piles of lumber. Order had come to the ribbon of earth along the road, where order had no place.

At the edge of this desolation stood Madan Babu, a Punjabi, the local road contractor. Hands on his hips, he was supervising the crew. Methodically, fifteen men and women laborers were moving down the right of way, wielding axes, crowbars, and sledge hammers.

I asked what was going on. Madan Babu told me that the road was being widened and that everything on the government right-of-way had to be removed. People had been given notice but had paid no heed. "Too bad," he said, spitting out his betel. "They didn't believe us."

I could see why. It would be very rash indeed to upset your business routine because a government circular said you would be moved. Anyway, the value of the stalls was not in their lumber, but in the location. They were planted in the middle of the market crowds, and they sold goods which the peasants bought on impulse. A man needed a mango worse standing sweaty shoulder to sweaty shoulder in the middle of an immobile crowd than he would have needed one in the open area under the tree. Logic dictated that the mango vendor seek the center of the crowd.

I asked Madan Babu when the road work would start. Who could tell? He already had one-half million rupees in unpaid bills, certainly nothing would be done until the election. Or, in his opinion, after. "These Biharis. They're all the same. Look at Karu Sao's new house. The balcony," he paused again to spit, "juts over the right of way. I have called the constables, and while they watch the laborers will climb up and knock the outer foot off the balcony. Karu Sao knew the road was to be widened when he built. So why didn't he measure? Because he is a fat "bania," a merchant, not a laborer. He lets the workment measure it. themselves. What do they care?"

These tirades upset me, partly because they were true. Hearing anti-Bihari sentiments from an Indian made it easier for me to fall back on them. I had to remind myself that India was not one, and that Madan Babu, fully as much as I, was a representative here of an outside culture.

K. P. Katriar stood to one side, smiling, his eyes narrow. I asked what he thought of the clearing. He said it was like a gift from the government: "Who will vote for them after they destroy property and livelihood this way?" He thought he had found his issue. Mr. Kumar, who was watching from his jeep, laughed when I told him this. "Poor K. P. Of course people are unhappy. All that means is that a few votes will go to the Raja. And K. P. won't make trouble when the balcony goes down. He only wants to harvest the outrage."

Nonetheless, Madan Babu had drawn up a line of fifteen constables to protect him. The laborers began to demolish the concrete apron in front of Karu Sao's house. People muttered but no one moved. I decided that nothing would happen except that the balcony would come down, and walked off to the post office.

When I returned, the workmen had left. Six inches of Karu Sao's balcony still jutted over the right of way. No doubt it had been time for Madan Babu's dinner. The next week all the stalls were back in their accustomed places on the roadway. Normalcy had reasserted itself.

It was growing chilly again, and the election was two weeks away. I wandered over to the mukhia's one February night and found him meeting with several officials of the local cooperative. The government put up the funds for these co-ops. The supervisors controlled the flow of loans and repayments to members. The mukhia was on the board of directors of the District Cooperative Bank, but they were not discussing the bank. They were discussing the part co-op officials could play in the campaign of Radha Gobind Prasad.

The mukhia began by apologizing for imposing on them. He assured them that his own involvement in the campaign reflected his deep desire to save Barhi from the ravages of the Raja. He was confident that they agreed and understood their responsibility.

Radha Gobind was clearly the best candidate. The Raja's son had never, the mukhia claimed, finished high school, while Radha Gobind was one of two men to get a Doctor of Laws from Patna University under the British. Radha Gobind had years of experience in the Assembly; had he represented Barhi during the famine, they would not have suffered while all relief aid went to other areas.

The co-op workers saved the mukhia any further explanations by assuring him that everyone was clearly working for the good of the community. The question of motives having been settled by mutual admiration, the group got down to brass tacks. They reviewed the key individual in each village, his financial situation, personal position, and relations with the cooperative.

The mukhia reminded them that he would never think of asking honest government servants like themselves to undertake anything unethical. They, of course, could not actually campaign for Radha Gobind. All he wanted was for them to explain, in their capacity as private citizens, the benefits to the community of a Congress victory. The chorus assented. They would educate, not campaign. Then everyone drank tea.

All present knew that everyone tried to use government officials in elections. I was surprised that it was a matter for such delicacy. Was the fig leaf for my benefit? I thought not. It was for theirs. And I was surprised that the mukhia, in front of me, had been so open about the negotiations. He had always boasted that he never resorted to the usual tactics of Bihari politics. I had never taken that seriously, but I had assumed that he meant me to. I had to conclude that the mukhia did not interpret his negotiations with the cooperative supervisors as "dirty politics."

The Congress brought its big guns to Bihar. The mukhia announced that Morarji Desai, Minister of Finance and Deputy Prime Minister, would speak in Barhi on his way to Hazaribagh. Congress workers scurried around, sending advance word to the villages, so that Desai's appearance would boost the campaign of Radha Gobind Prasad. Congress cadres perched on uncertain ladders to hang garlands of mango leaves over the highway, while others erected a small platform in the field where Desai would speak.

The day before Desai was due, Jagdish asked Judy, "Memsahib, who is this big man who is coming to speak?"

Judy told Jagdish that his name was Morarji Desai and that he was Deputy Prime Minister of India.

"So he is a very important man?"

"Why yes. Very important. Are you going?"

"Yes, Memsahib. Such people don't come to Barhi often. But will I be able to understand him?"

Judy laughed, "Yes, he is coming to speak to villagers, so he will speak the language of the villages. But go early. There will be a big crowd."

The next morning Jagdish consulted me about the day's shopping. When we had finished, he scratched his head and finally asked, "Sahib, is this man who is speaking today an American?"

I looked up, startled. "No, what made you think that?"

"Well," he said logically, "you and Memsahib knew all about him and my family had never heard of him. I thought he might be from your country." He paused, "Is he an Indian?"

"Yes, Jagdish. He is Deputy Prime Minister of India. That means he sits right next to Indira Ghandi."

"Next to Nehruji's daughter! He must be very important."

A great crowd lined the road that afternoon. Out front B. P. Katriar stood anxiously, waving his arms at the two small girls who were carrying garlands for Desai, cocking one eye at the mango laurels hung over the road, speculating whether they would stay up in the wind, running across the road to reposition the band, barking orders to the constables to clear the way, finally relaxing for a moment to look down the road for the motorcade.

When Desai arrived, the mukhia escorted him to the platform, introduced him, and sat back with a quiet smile while Desai described the failures of the anti-Congress coalition, the waste of relief funds during the famine, the villainy of the anti-Congress leaders, and the certain ruin for everyone if they regained power.

Jagdish reported his conclusions at dinner. It was, he thought, a very good speech, a much better speech than the one the Raja used to give, which was all about himself. Jagdish's decision to vote for the Congress had, we gathered, been confirmed. But before he left he had to ask once more what the speaker's name had been.

Next morning I met a peasant repairing his thorn hedge near Champadih. He would vote for the Raja's son. I pressed him for reasons. What had the Raja's son done for the area? Had he come around to see how people were doing during the famine? The man was stubborn. He was not concerned with that. He would vote for the Raja, and his son.

He pointed to a man coming down the lane. "Ask him," he urged me, "who is he going to vote for?" The man stopped for a moment, looked at one of the bundles of thorn piled by the hedge. He reached over, twisted off one thorn and used it to pick his teeth. Then he threw down the thorn and gazed at the horizon. "I have eaten the Raja's salt," he said, and walked away. It was, for both of them, the definitive political philosophy.

Although the election cramped our more ambitious plans, Ram Sewak and I made our rounds of the block by bicycle. I met him in the morning with condoms, pamphlets, and the large yellow posters that I had finally rescued from the mildew on the shelf.

One day he asked me to leave our supplies behind, for he planned to spend the day supervising the Kariatpur staff. Dr. Agarwal had passed that responsibility on to him, and Ram Sewak was proud of it. It compensated for Dr. Agarwal's rather military manner, which offended Ram Sewak's egalitarian dignity.

I insisted on taking the yellow posters, though Ram Sewak laughingly asked me, "Do you know how long they stay up? Every school child in Barhi has a book cover made out of one by now."

When we got to Kariatpur and told Mandel that Ram Sewak was going to inspect his work, Mandel immediately took the offensive. "Is that all? I'm here alone, people insult me, the doctor gives me targets. You ought to help me—all we get is supervision and harassment. Now you join the line!" I rested my forehead on my hand, shielding my eyes. Ram Sewak's willing spirit had spoiled me. I knew that Mandel was a victim but did not want to hear his complaints.

When his rhetoric was exhausted, Mandel sat down to await Ram Sewak's inspection. "Mandelji," Ram Sewak began, "where are the condoms you take to the village?"

"At the center," Mandel lied.

"How many men are taking them?"

"Two or three."

Ram Sewak pointed out that in their spare time the school-teachers were managing to find eight or nine men in single villages to use them. Mandel had full time and the range of twenty or so villages. As he and Ram Sewak talked, Ram Sewak calm and questioning, Mandel cutting back and forth between strident protestations that it wasn't possible and silent pleadings to be left alone, I realized how little I had contributed to Barhi's family planning program. Ram Sewak and I did a good job in the meetings we conducted personally. But, in fact, Ram Sewak did such a good job that he didn't need me at all. And as he had shown with Olivia Dhan, Ram Sewak could mediate between the staff members' traditional background and the bureaucracy of the English world. He could not get them to translate for themselves, though; and more important, he could not insulate them from the Health Ministry with its hostility toward the lower level staff, its assumption that they did not work, and its elaborate machinery of harassment. Ram Sewak himself was not free, as shown by the need to spend a whole day looking at bogus registers with Mandel.

We were all the victims of a euphemism. The family planning program had little to do with family planning. The Health Ministry had only marginally more to do with health. Both seemed, in the light of a year in Barhi, to be many other things. They were social security systems for their employees, sources of patronage for politicians, extensions and aggrandizements of the British-spawned civil service, emergency employment projects for the educated unemployed, a surety offered to inquisitive foreign governments that pressured the Indian government to undertake certain favorite "development" schemes.

I had become a participant in a vast public works and employment program, which for reasons of ritual hired only staff with medical training. Ram Sewak and I needed to work outside this machinery. The condom scheme was one way, but it was very limited. It solved the supply problem and left the demand problem untouched. Perhaps the villagers would only plan their families when changes in agriculture, in politics, in education brought the word "planning" into daily use. Perhaps family planning should be abandoned altogether as an idea whose time had not yet come.

I left Ram Sewak peering at Mandel's illegible scrawl and tacked posters against the walls of a school. The children watched me greedily. Next door, two bullocks turned round and round over the harvested rice. A puff of dust rose in the winter sun. They would still be threshing at night fall. Only a random step brought their hooves down on the unthreshed grain. Ram Sewak and I were teaching a few people at random meetings. But chance was not good enough in Barhi. It got lost in all the other chances, in the randomness the old man in the railway station thought applied to train schedules, because it applied to everything else in his life. Barhi deserved something better than the odd chance. Ram Sewak deserved something better from me.

Ram Sewak had often talked of the possibilities of politics, but the election made me dubious. I didn't think I should be expressing an opinion, but I was used to having one. This time I didn't have one. Perhaps the indifferent peasant was right: What choice could make a difference?

The villagers saw the election as a game of the rich in which they were pawns but pawns with a stake. Their votes had a certain market value—jobs for members of their caste, a road for the village, blankets from the Raja. The candidates came from the traditional ruling groups: both B. P. and K. P. Katriar were Brahmins, the Raja a Kshatriya. No untouchable candidate asked Jagdish for his vote, no small cultivator appealed to the vegetable growers of Kariatpur. The people could sell but not buy.

All this was open. No one had to explain to Jagdish how caste had destroyed his father, or show the villagers of Karso village how their mukhia had stolen their land through usury. He solicited their votes in every village election on exactly that basis.

No party challenged this system. The Jana Sangh wanted to restore the patterns of the past. Its welfare slogans and promises were no more central to the villagers' interests than the blankets he gave away were to the Raja's manipulation of government mining contracts. The Congress meant B. P. Katriar. Like others I depended on him personally; I admired his wit and good sense. Yet I had visited a village near the Grand Trunk Road that could not get its crops to market because the land between the village and the road was owned by the mukhia, who refused permission to build a road on it. He promised, of course, that if Radha Gobind Prasad won the election the government would buy land for the road.

Traveling back from that village, angry, I listened to Ram Sewak's political philosophy. He was a communist, not a party hack like the members of the Communist Party of India, but a "real communist."

Since Ram Sewak was also proud to be a landowner, what did a "real communist" mean? "Why, it means that if I have a field and a man plows and works it for me and I get two bushels of rice, I should give him one bushel." It was the old Ghandian ideal that I had cherished, the trusteeship of the rich. How much could that, or any other idea, change Barhi? No party wanted to deal with poverty, disease, or illiteracy. The Jana Sangh turned to religion, the Congress to caste, the Raja to tradition. The parties were an expression of the dilemma, not instruments to resolve it.

The elite in Barhi were fond of pointing this out, gleefully assuring us that in politics, "it's all a matter of caste and religion, not the man or the issue." They oversimplified, out of nostalgia for simpler days when instead of caste politics there had simply been caste. Everyone at the top agreed that the village elections for mukhia had "injected rotten factionalism into the village." "Before there was unity," they said, "now there is feuding. The mukhias are elected because they control the votes, and they control votes because they are rich. They are not the real leaders."

For those at the top, the opening up of competition was an unpromising innovation. The old village unity had been the unity of their unchallenged monopoly. Now that monopoly, even the Raja's, was being challenged. The Raja had begun to worry. He moved in vigorously. The helicopter dropped on village after village, blankets reached more and more families. Dr. Agarwal was convinced the Raja would win. "He spends fantastically, outrageously. He has put fifty thousand rupees into this one constituency alone. Think of what he must be putting out for the whole district!"

Common sense dictated that the villagers sell their votes. But why stay bought? Why the traditional honesty implied by the statement "I have eaten the Raja's salt"? New institutions, even the schools, were commonly thought to lack traditional integrity. Schoolteachers were rumored to have sold the powdered milk supplied for their pupils during the famine, but no one suspected the mullahs of stealing the alms of the faithful. The innovation of the vote was seen as an extension of traditional ways; eating the salt still had meaning to the voter if not to the Raja.

Election day was warm for February. It was an official holi-

143

day. The polling station had been set up at the Middle School, a shaded building left over from colonial times. Children sat on the banisters joking or played around the school well. But their real attention was fixed on the three tables in front of the building and on the voting booth formed of hanging sheets.

The election clerks sat behind one desk, backed by an observer from each party. Each voter received his ballot and the special pen used to place an X next to the symbol of his party. He disappeared behind the sheets, marked his ballot, and deposited it in the metal box. It was orderly. People waited in lines. Everyone knew his duty, the path to the booth had been laid out with strings.

Ritual was something these people loved and understood. Few of them knew what happened to their paper ballot after they dropped it in the box. Many may have imagined that the act of dropping itself cause the vote to be recorded. But they were very careful to perform the rite as they had been instructed.

The polling officials, who understood the whole process, laughed and joked, gossiped about the outlook, and exchanged political invective. The people stood quietly; one or two slipped off their shoes before entering the polling area, and when they had cast their votes they hurried away softly from the sacred precinct.

It took several days for the results to drift back to Barhi. Arun and Morari Katriar went into Hazaribagh each day to see if the Barhi ballots had been counted. They feared they had lost. The night after the election the mukhia held a postmortem. Congress Party workers from all over the block drifted in. The mukhia, reclining on the sofa, received each bit of intelligence with an impatient nod of the head, "Yes, yes, go on. Can't you be more specific?" But the tales were specific enough: the Raja's name and spending had told heavily even in the strongest Congress villages.

Finally word came. The Raja's son had taken more votes than the combined opposition. The Janata Party had swept all its usual strongholds in the Hazaribagh District. But Morari, who brought the news, was smiling as he told us.

"He's won this time, but there's no question his influence is gone. He had to buy this election. Now its a matter of time. He passed the courthouse in Hazaribagh today in his car with the party flag. Some of his men tried to get the crowd to applaud him. They started the chant 'Raja Bahadur Kamakya Narain Singh ki' and no one gave the 'Jai!' ('Long Live!'). He's on his way out, uprooted, demolished!"

The cabinet which emerged from the election, the "Second United Front," fell apart in a few months when the Minister of Mines, one Kamakya Narain Singh, demanded of the Chief Minister that certain cases over mineral rights pending in the high court against one Raja of Ramgarh be dropped. The Chief Minister, an honest or a timid man, resigned in protest, and Barhi returned to administrative rule from New Delhi—from Kiranni Raj back to Kiranni Raj.

"Two hundred thousand rupees they spent on that election," Dr. Agarwal remarked, "that's five thousand rupees a day for every day the cabinet lasted." He did not seem surprised.

13. Ram Sewak and I did less traveling as the heat of early March came upon us. I spent more time with the Katriars, and one evening I found Shobha alone in the kitchen, kneeling beside the coal fire and stirring up a great mass of thick bread dough with a wooden spoon.

"Namaste, Shobhaji," I called out. "Is your father in?"

"No," she answered, "he's gone to Patna."

"Wedding business?" I joked. The mukhia had turned from full-time campaigning to full-time matchmaking. He was determined to marry Shobha before the monsoon, and equally determined to make it the biggest wedding Barhi had ever seen. She was his youngest daughter and it would be his last chance to stage a spectacle.

"Are you going to meet the man first—before they decide, or before you marry him?"

"No."

"Don't you want to?" I needled her.

"Not really. I trust mama and papa. They may show me a picture, they may not. What do I know about it?"

"What do you know about it? Shobha, you're going to spend the rest of your life with this man and you're not even curious. I do *not* understand this system. The poor parents can hardly manage to find someone, the poor sons and daughters get married off, and everyone says 'that's how it is.' "

"That's very true," she said. "I will be very happy if my own children make love marriages. But if the parents really love the children, don't you think they should take some interest?"

"Interest, maybe," I said, "But arrange the whole thing? It turns into a business deal, dowry here, dowry there, buying and selling, just to get married."

"*That* is bad." She wiped her face with the back of her hand and patted her long hair into place. She reminded me of her mother; the same energy was there, underneath Shobha's genial manner. "The dowries ruin our families—that won't last. If the times change, I certainly wouldn't want any of my children involved with dowry. But people here are so greedy. Did you know there was a committee in Hazaribagh once, to eliminate the dowry?"

"No, what happened to it?"

"Oh, all the important people joined it. They signed a pledge: 'We will not give dowry with our daughters, nor accept it for our sons.' Then they all hurried around and married off their daughters first. When the groom's father would ask for dowry, they would point to the pledge. Then, when all the daughters were safely married, they dissolved the committee and took dowry for their sons." She smiled. Her scorn was good-natured.

I thought of the morning before when I had been cycling at six o'clock to meet Ram Sewak. I had passed Shobha in back of the cold storage plant, brushing her teeth with a twig. It was probably the only time of day when she was alone and free of the house. How would she feel about exchanging the protected position of youngest daughter for the exposed and rocky one of daughter-in-law?

When Shobha and her sisters went to the movies, Morari's wife had to stay home and keep house. After fourteen months of seeing Morari's wife almost daily, I still didn't know her name.

"Shobha, what is your sister-in-law's name?"

"You don't know?"

"No. I don't know why. I can't remember anyone using it,"

"No one here ever would. She's a member of the family! I call her sister-in-law, Morari calls her wife, the children call her mother."

"You never use names in the family?"

"No."

"Why not?"

"Why should we? We know who we mean."

She was right. And now that I thought about it, it made

sense. Roles, titles, dominated the household, structured it. Any daughter-in-law had the same duties, must bring tea with the same meek regularity, cover her head with the sari in the presence of her father-in-law, and accept the least pleasant cleaning chores. Her name didn't matter; her individuality would have to be fitted into the nooks and crannies of household life.

"Shobha, when you get married, will the pandit use your name and the name of your husband?"

She sat back from the smoky fire and thought for a moment. "No. The ceremony is always the same. For everybody. It never changes."

The mukhia returned from Patna, having fixed Shobha's wedding for the end of May. Shobha would not see a picture. The mukhia commented on his age, this might be the last chance to marry Shobha, the wedding would be big. Ram Sewak was sure he meant it. The Kaysthe Brahmins, the Katriars' caste, had a reputation for extravagance, wheras Ram Sewak's own Bhoomiar group were frugal and thrifty. According to Ram Sewak, one Kaysthe merchant in Jhumri Tilaiya had ruined himself marrying a daughter. When the guests arrived at the party they complained that they were expected to drink water out of the well, instead of being provided with lemonade as was the custom. Their host bade them haul up a bucket and taste. He had turned every well in the village but one into a lemonade well.

I was no longer polite on this subject. In the midst of these filthy lanes, poor men and women purchased thin silver and gold foil to cover sweets at the weddings of their undernourished and underclothed children. "It's wrong, Ram Sewak, to spend money that way!"

Ram Sewak sighed. "Ah, yes, Pope Sahib, that's the way it is."

Judy asked Shobha why that was the way. "It's the times," Shobha said.

"But who are the times, Shobha? Who makes them?"

"People."

"Isn't your father one of the people?" She had covered this ground over a hundred cups of tea.

"Yes, but only one. What can one man do?"

In the case of B. P. Katriar, one man could do quite a lot. "I tell you, Mr. Pope, this wedding will set me back at least thirty thousand chips!" He smacked his bald pate with the palm of his hand. "Look at prices. Milk at one and one-half rupees, meat at four rupees, rice at two rupees—everything goes up, but everything will be the finest. You and Judy will see a real wedding. Elephants, bands, banners, dancing. I want to show you all the things which go into a traditional Kaysthe wedding. You know they are going out."

He paused, uncertain of his own feelings, the traditionalist father and the modern businessman at war. "Really people are more sensible these days. When I was young, the groom's party came a full week before the wedding. Now in two days it will be over. No one has the time . . ." He trailed off, then brightened. "Thirty thousand chips, Mr. Pope!"

Judy and I tried to imagine what the groom would be like. We wondered for Shobha's sake. We feared the mukhia would pick another mild-mannered clerk. Each of his sons-in-law, through the mukhia's careful selection or through the sheer force of his personality, had taken a subsidiary place in the Katriar hierarchy. The Bihari custom was that daughters went to live with their fathers-in-law. The mukhia respected the form of this rule, but in fact all his daughters spent their time in the house at Barhi, often with their husbands. I suspected that Shobha's husband, however worthy, would not challenge B. P. Katriar's hold over his daughter.

The father-in-law, however, might. Shobha was much more worried about her in-laws than her husband. Suppose the father-in-law had the drive of the mukhia? A little black corner in our hearts would have enjoyed watching someone challenge B. P.'s sovereignty. But we would not know for two months.

14. As I sat at the dining room table making sets of flash cards for the staff, I heard a timid knock at the door. I was glad of the interruption. Each set of flashcards I had made since coming to Barhi had been simpler than the last. The present set was unbelievably stylized and easy to use. But it had to be used *for* something, something being a brief talk on human reproduction, and so far none of the staff except Ram Sewak had been willing to give such a talk.

I was filling time, adding an hour or so to the three hours of field work that Ram Sewak and I managed in the March heat. That made a four-hour day. Well, maybe the visitor would enable me to put in a grueling four and a half. I opened the door.

The man who stood there was no shorter than most Biharis. But his thin face and limbs made him seem frail. He smiled nervously, waiting for me to speak.

"Namaste. Can I help you?"

"You are Mr. Pope? he said in hesitant English.

I nodded and told him in Hindi that he did not have to speak English. He scratched his head and said that he was a Bengali and would rather speak English than Hindi. He had heard that we were Christians and had come to talk. I invited him in. He joined me at the table and folded his hands in front of his face.

I offered him a glass of water, which he declined. Finally he said, "I have come about Easter."

Was Easter coming up?

He wanted to know if, perhaps, we would be bringing a minister to Barhi to conduct Easter services? Had the British brought

ministers out to conduct services? Then I remembered that
Hindu families did exactly this when they hired a priest to conduct prayers at social functions and on religious holidays. I explained to him that we would not be bringing a minister. Why
had he asked?

"I, too, am a Christian you see. I thought it might be nice if
we had services here in Barhi once." He asked what we would do
on Easter. Not wishing to tell him that we were not religious, I
said we might go into Hazaribagh to the Mission Church. He
smiled. I asked what he did. He was an electrical engineer at the
substation outside Barhi. I waited for the usual questions: Do
you grow rice in your country? Is it hot there? How do you like
India?

He asked none of them, but after a few minutes of rather
awkward silence got up and left.

Later, walking in the bazaar, I met the timid Bengali carrying
a basket of eggplant. I forgot and addressed him in Hindi; he
corrected me. I asked why Bengalis were so sticky about speaking
English.

"Oh, no, it is not like that, it is not that I am not liking
Hindi," he protested, looking around nervously at his Hindi-
speaking neighbors, "it is that I am not speaking it very well." I
could hardly understand his English, but perhaps his Hindi was
worse.

"Will you and your missus come and have tea with us?" he
said, waving his hands at a flock of small children who were dart-
ing around his legs. I accepted and he told me how to find his
house.

Before we parted he turned and grinned broadly. "I work the
'hot lines,'" he said enigmatically, and was promptly swallowed
up in the crowd.

At tea time the following evening the Bengali met us on his
front porch and with a grand gesture waved at his half of the
duplex house. His eyes were wondering if I would laugh if he
said, "Welcome to our home." So instead he pointed apologetic-
ally to the humming substation and said: "It is a big problem;
sometimes we cannot sleep because of the noise. I am entitled,"
he paused over the word, "*entitled* to a class-two quarter, and
this is only a class-three quarter, but they don't do anything
about it."

151

All his children had their hair cut in pageboys. I had become accustomed to cropped hair on boys and long braids on girls.

We sat on the porch in the same straightbacked wooden chairs one found in every government office, headman's hut, and business, from Calcutta to Bombay. The Bengali asked his children to bring us tea, and his wife brought a plate of cookies. He told us that his wife spoke no English, so would we mind speaking Hindi. The gesture was quite unusual; most men in Barhi who spoke English wanted to show off and refused to let us switch into Hindi, though their wives who spoke no English were present.

His Hindi, it developed, was quite good. We discovered that his children's haircut was not the only thing that separated him from his neighbors. He had the first real imagination I had encountered in Barhi. He actually speculated on what life in the United States might be like and he tried his guesses out on us. He talked directly to Judy and carefully included his wife in the conversation.

After tea he showed us a faded group portrait of the class in engineering school where he had been trained. One Westerner sat amidst the Indians. He pointed to him with pride. This was his "American expert," a Mr. Harkness, who had trained him in the "hot-line work." I remembered his enigmatic remark in the bazaar and asked what "hot-line work" meant. I warned him that I knew little about electronics. He explained that hot-line operators could conduct maintenance and repair on transmission wires while they were still live; when a break occurred, it was not necessary to shut off power to the whole grid. It was, he said, very dangerous. I could believe it.

Then he paused. "But I do not get to do it. They do not have the equipment for the work. At Dhanbad they have it, and I have tried for three years to get a transfer, but it is not coming. They do not even answer my letters." He rested his head on his hands.

We tried to comfort him, but he explained that this was the reason he had a class-three instead of a class-two house. For two years he had been in Barhi doing nothing. Every day he went to the office where, since he was not an office worker, he did not have a desk. He ran a few errands and returned to his house.

"I stay at home and educate the children. They do not speak Hindi, there is no Bengali school here. I teach them to write, to read. I show them geography." He pointed to a large paper globe in the corner of the porch, which he had cut out of a magazine and pasted together for his son. I was confident it was the only globe in Barhi. I was about to compliment him on it, when he continued, "I help my wife, and do the marketing, but I do not have real work."

We sat quietly in the dark. The children dashed about the fenced-in yard, chasing butterflies. The Bengali reminded me of Jagdish, but he lacked Jagdish's tough peasant spirit. I could see how he had been broken by idleness, and I could understand why he seemed wary of Barhi. I supposed that the last good thing in his life had been his training with Mr. Harkness. But he was too high-strung, too much of a dreamer for Barhi.

His wife had gone inside to put the children to bed. Now she came back and invited us to dinner. I could not face more time with them at that moment. We begged off, saying that Jagdish had already prepared food, that he would be waiting. The Bengali walked us to the gate.

As soon as my feet touched the asphalt pavement I understood that the invitation to tea had also been an invitation to dinner, that his wife had prepared food especially for us. Everything I had learned screamed out that we should turn back and accept their invitation. I wanted to, but I couldn't. As we went down the road the guilt and regret grew stronger, but it also became more awkward to turn around. Inertia was carrying me back to our house, to a dinner with Judy with the curtains closed against Barhi.

"We should have stayed. She made a meal for us, I know it. Now she thinks we don't want to eat with them because they are poor. Why didn't we see?"

Judy didn't answer except to squeeze my hand. "Do you want to go back?" We walked more slowly and at one point I nearly did stop, but the rebuff, the insult, had already been delivered. I had been threatened by the Bengali and his story. No, I had been threatened by Barhi, by fifteen months here. I was trying to stay afloat.

I thought of the flashcards I had been making the day the Bengali first came. Were they, like the little paper globe, a substitute for real work?

There was real work with Ram Sewak, but it was his, not mine. I was a companion for the road. Our friendship was nourished by the shared satisfactions of our monthly condom distributions, of our meetings in the villages where the men looked at the flashcards describing human reproduction and then asked the village priest to confirm or deny this strange story. When we cycled together into a market the children called after us, "Two or three children—enough!" The posters ended up as book covers, but the publicity had been made. Barhi had heard of family planning.

But I needed a sense that something would happen after I left, and I didn't have it. I began to run down. There was that same heaviness when I got up in the morning that I had felt in the last hot season. Now it was not climate, not the food or disease that wore me down after four hours. The inertia on all sides was a giant short-circuit. Its causes were everywhere, and they were also its result: sloppy agriculture, bad nutrition, poor education, crowding. Judy and I told ourselves that our ideas were seeds, our example fertilizer; new ideas could take root and grow. Only that kind of metaphor could justify what we did, but the metaphor was inappropriate. The men, the animals, even the plants were like unpowered gears, levers, wheels. Every new idea had to be weighed against the energy required to carry it forward. I could go to the office, see a letter typed, drink tea with the typist, help him proof it, watch it being signed and stamped, seal the envelope, return it to the clerk for entry in the dispatch log, place it in the "out" box. I would come back a week later and find it in the same place.

Physical and emotional weakness led people to conserve their interests, their efforts. They had no margin for risk. They could not afford new ideas, even ones that were economically "free."

I too was withdrawing, trying to insulate myself from possible failure. I would leave the envelope in the "out" box instead of mailing it myself. That way, in a week, there would still be something simple I could do, and it would be a week longer before I knew that the minister in Patna had no intention of answering it.

I had spent over a year assaulting Barhi bureaucracy. Now I confined myself to a prayer that the whole machinery would disappear, leaving Judy and me and Dr. Agarwal and Dr. Malik and Ram Sewak to run a local program.

Dr. Malik waited for gasoline money that never came. Letters to Patna went unanswered. Finally Brij Bansi Prasad himself came on an inspection of Barhi. Dr. Malik confronted him. He cavalierly told her that she should run the jeep out of her own pocket. "Tour in the national spirit," he said.

I questioned Brij Bansi's driver. Oh, yes, Sahib was always careful to draw his travel allowance.

Dr. Malik went to Patna and arranged a transfer to a large hospital.

Sitting at the bus stop with Ram Sewak I would pray that the bus would not come. One passed, the driver refused to take us; I would grumble with Ram Sewak about the arrogance of bus drivers, but inside I was glad. We would resume our wait in the dusty shade. A second bus came. Ram Sewak talked with the conductor, an honest one this time, and we would grab the underframes of our cycles, hoist them on top of the bus, and rattle off to a rendezvous.

Ram Sewak did not understand my mood. We were not to blame for the failings of Brij Bansi Prasad. We did the best we could. But this was no longer enough for me.

"Everything above us in this program is bogus, Pope Sahib, and the villages are slow and backward. But we do our jobs."

His idea of duty and integrity came from the Gita: "Concern yourself with right action, not with the fruits of action." His knowledge that he did well under the circumstances gave him a comfort I could not find. Arriving in a village, he called together the leaders, sprawled on the cot, and tailored his style to theirs. He saw that these speeches did not meet the needs of the peasants, that his talents and training in medicine were wasted—but his comment, "Pope Sahib, if you and I could really do something for these people . . ." contained the stoic recognition that "this is not to be."

If it was not, I had to ask myself "Why am I staying here?"

In late March some men broke into the house of the local Inspector of Police and stole the money he had put away for his daughter's marriage. Red-capped constables went through nearly every house in town, beating up a dozen men and women and arresting nine. Police dogs converged on Barhi to trace the thieves and their loot. By a narrow vote the dogs picked an old well as the end of the trail, so in the first few weeks of the hot season, with water already scarce, the police hauled in diesel pumps and emptied the well. When the water was gone, the well, alas, was empty.

Local gossip claimed that the inspector had lost 100,000 rupees. The inspector said he had lost 12,000. This showed what people thought of the behavior of the police. The inspector made about 600 rupees monthly. Twelve thousand rupees represented the highest sum he could have saved legitimately. Above that, the higher a value you placed on the robbery, the lower the value you set on the inspector's honesty.

The police angered Barhi. Ram Sewak and I canceled one family planning movie because it conflicted with a protest delegation to Mr. Kumar. The organizers felt that too many people would watch the movie instead of protesting. We stopped a second showing when a rock was thrown at the projector. Someone was trying to insure that the town remain upset about the beatings.

"Someone" turned out to be K. P. Katriar. The Jana Sangh leader expressed his sorrow to me that none of the suspects had died of their beating. It would, to his mind, have made agitation easier. I went away from our discussion trembling. It was the first time I had hated anyone in Barhi. But whatever my reaction to K. P.'s exploitation of the robbery, I sympathized with the popular mood. The police had no evidence against the men they had arrested. The town was sure they were innocent. They had been picked up because they all frequented a tea stall with a recently fired driver who had worked with the inspector. Unfortunately for the police, the nine included one tribal villager, one Brahmin, two Muslims, a local Christian, and several members of local peasant castes. The driver was a Nepali. Everyone agreed that these nine could never have conspired to do *anything* together. Mrs. Srivastava pointed out that they would have had to consult different astrologers about the propitious night for the theft.

I stopped drinking tea with the police constables. The nine men, I knew, were still in jail, although several had good alibis. I wanted to show that I shared the people's feelings. No one noticed that I was not drinking tea with the constables, not even the constables. When I told Ram Sewak he laughed heartily.

About two weeks after the theft Ram Sewak and I rode out

to a distant village where the talk was all of the 100,000-rupee robbery and the "shameful" police behavior. Every man in the village had some piece of gossip about how the inspector had amassed his lost fortune. The headman asked if this kind of thing happened in the United States.

I said that it did happen on occasion, but that we had appeal procedures to protect people against false arrest, and that popular outcry after such incidents was often very great. Sometimes, I said rather optimistically, we even managed to punish the police.

"That's good," the headman said, nodding his white cowlick in approval. "I tell you, the police have come to a sorry state. They arrest and beat up innocent people." Everyone agreed. I recalled the mukhia's cynical remark. "In your country Mr. Pope, the police investigate so they may find suspects. Here, we arrest so that we may investigate." It was reassuring to find that most people did not endorse that procedure.

The villagers began to discuss police behavior in general. Each had a nugget of gossip about the robbery, each contributed his favorite police atrocity story. When the last man finished his tale, everyone turned to the headman to sum up.

He looked at me, the American in Indian khadi, sitting on a string cot under a straw roof with visions of due process and presumptions of innocence dancing in his head, while he, the village headman by choice, squatted on his heels in the dust.

"Sahib," he said, "it was much better in the old days. Then the police never went after the innocent, they pursued only the guilty, but when they caught them, there was none of this trial and jail business. They simply chopped off their hands. We need police like that."

Everyone nodded.

15.   Our condom program never recovered from its holiday excesses before Holi. These excesses consisted of Ram Sewak and me having taken the letter of the government rules about condoms—which advocated free and easy supply, instead of the spirit—which held that each condom must be carefully recorded at each stage of its journey from manufacturer to dung heap. Since some of these steps were beyond the purview of government clerks and were not incorporated in the simple forms we had given the schoolteachers to keep, Dr. Gope refused to supply us with condoms for April.

He said it was too bad, but he could not issue condoms for us until we turned in a report for the previous month indicating how many of the men we supplied used the condoms regularly, and how many irregularly. He told us that he had sent an order to that effect that very morning. I pointed out, first, that he had never been able to define what constituted a "regular" user or how we might find out who used his condoms regularly. He looked blank. Then I objected that the schoolteachers came in only one day of the month, and that it was impossible to gather records from them on that day *and* to supply those records the week before when we came in to pick up the condoms.

He was deeply sorry. He didn't believe the condoms were being properly used anyway. (What Dr. Gope meant by "improper" use, I was never able to figure out.) So we would have to submit a report. Perhaps I could ask the teachers to file advance reports by mail. In fact, they were not doing enough reporting anyway. And, then and there he added three new columns to the report they had to submit.

He resolutely refused to supply me with condoms.

We had to put all the schoolteachers on short rations that month, which turned out not to matter, since they all planned to take it easy in April to recover from the "excesses" of Holi. They were sure their friends who used condoms would be doing the same. Even Chaudhrikar Mahato, who always wanted 144 condoms, was content with 30.

Shortly after, Ram Sewak met me at the hospital with a worried look. We had to start getting proper records from the schoolteachers. What we had been doing—my writing down whatever the schoolteachers told me—was not good enough. It was insane, but in another block they had just fined the Extension Educator 500 rupees for inadequate records.

"Who told you this?"

"Dr. Agarwal."

We walked over to the doctor's house.

Dr. Agarwal sighed. "Both the doctor and the Extension Educator in the block have been fined 500 rupees for incomplete records. There is no question of their having stolen anything, they just didn't keep all the records. They had their three-year audit, and when they couldn't present evidence of where each and every condom had gone the auditor fined them."

I tried to control myself, succeeded for ten seconds, then blew up. "It's God-damn *illegal* to do your job in this system! Schoolteachers aren't government clerks. We can't ask them to be. This program is the only thing that works at all!"

Having exploded, I found myself resigned to trying to keep the records. Five hundred rupees was two months' salary for Ram Sewak. I could fake records and vanish with them at the end of two years. I couldn't ask Dr. Agarwal and Ram Sewak to do that; they would be here for the auditor.

To my astonishment, Chaudrikhar Mahato brought his register to the next meeting. I dutifully examined it, feeling the fool. It was a farce. If Chaudrikhar wanted the condoms for some obscure, illegal purpose, he could have invented the names in the register. I congratulated him and gave him his cherished gross of condoms. Then Ram Sewak warned the rest that if they did not bring their registers he would quit distributing. Ten or twelve of the teachers immediately wanted to know how many condoms they had received to date, "just so I can check my register." This was promising. If they went to the trouble of fabricating records we might be able to conduct two programs. One would distribute condoms in the villages on a rather irregular basis when people needed or wanted them; the other would make up neat figures in registers. We gave out 2400 condoms, almost up to our Holi record.

But supplies were strained. Dr. Gope still refused to issue condoms unless the head clerk certified that our reports had been received and entered. When we filed reports, only about one in four was entered; the rest remained unprocessed until their purpose had been forgotten, at which point someone shuffled them a bit and slipped them into new files.

Judy and I decided to bypass the obstruction by going to Patna for supplies. Unexpectedly, we managed to fill our order directly from the state warehouse, which had no idea that monthly reports were a necessary prerequisite. We loaded the crates of condoms on a bus to Barhi.

I missed the next payday for the schoolteachers but asked Ram Sewak how many condoms he had distributed.

He looked sad. "Only two hundred and fifty, Pope Sahib. The schoolteachers all said that no one wanted condoms any more, that they couldn't give them away. The real reason is the records. The teachers do not want to keep the records, and they are afraid of punishment if they do not. What can we do?"

I kicked my bicycle tire. I was torn between my annoyance at Dr. Gope and my annoyance at the schoolteachers. They could have kept the records if they had been able to see the benefits of their work. But the only results were children not born into hunger, or mothers who would not die in childbirth. I began to feel like Sisyphus; I would push a project up a hill, almost to the crest, but at the top there was Dr. Gope, or the clerks, or the ministry to send it crashing to the bottom.

As if this were not enough, the hot weather had returned with a vengeance. April had been remarkably cool, with unexpected showers. As we dragged into May I felt the heat more than I had the first year. I was becoming unacclimated. And the heat was driving me from the daily work with Ram Sewak and the meager satisfaction of duty done.

Then word came that Dr. Gope was coming for an inspection

of the block. Normally Dr. Agarwal prepared for inspections. Charts were drawn up, elaborate summaries prepared, and particularly inept staff sent on leave to avoid the embarrassment of cross-examination. But with Dr. Gope, no preparation would work; no one knew what frenzy would possess him on a given day. It mattered little how well the staff answered his questions. He never heard them.

Dr. Gope's jeep arrived forty minutes late, practically on time. He bounced out of the vehicle with a hearty welcome for everyone. He always greeted us with a winning smile. It had taken several meetings for me to realize that his smile was the end of the relationship, not the beginning. He never noticed the person that he greeted and hardly remembered a face.

He clumped into the hospital and began the oration. To Ram Sewak's relief, today he was concerned with mother and child care and the work of the female staff. Dr. Agarwal, Judy, and I joined him in the parlor of Dr. Agarwal's house after he had looked at the records. There, over tea, Dr. Gope one by one summoned the nurses and midwives.

Mrs. Srivastava brought in her tattered records and placed them on the table. She tugged her sari nervously, bent over and straightened out the registers, never looking at Dr. Gope.

"Well, go on," he ordered, "open them up and show me what's in them."

"Yes, sir," she stammered and opened at random to the middle of the book. "Here is my register of pregnant women receiving antenatal care."

Dr. Gope peered through his thick glasses at one line. "Now where's this patient from? Barhi it says. Now this next case . . . this next case is from Konra. Now why are they all mixed up like this? How can you work that way?"

Mrs. Srivastava tried to explain that the women were entered chronologically, and that it was easy when she visited a village to look through and find the names of the patients from that area. Then Dr. Gope began to object that she should not be taking cases from so many villages.

"Why go to Konra when there must be other cases in Barhi which you are not visiting? Why spread yourself thin?"

Dr. Agarwal reassured him. In fact Konra was part of Barhi, and Mrs. Srivastava worked only in the immediate Barhi area.

"I don't agree with you, sir," Dr. Gope objected. "She should be working in the area right around the hospital, not wandering off to Konra."

"But, sir, the hospital itself is in Konra. Konra is just one of the neighborhoods of Barhi."

"Let me make myself clear, Doctor. We want to provide intensive services, not spread our staff all over the landscape."

He finished his tea, rose, hustled out the door. The last sight we had of Dr. Gope was of elbows waving and head bouncing up and down in the front of the jeep.

What led Dr. Gope to flit about the countryside, always cheerful except when challenged, always genial except when faced with facts, trailing commands and injunctions and orders behind him like wedding confetti, was the outcome of the whole structure within which Judy and I had lived for a year and a half.

The dominance of the red-stained corridors of the secretariat with their sullen clerks, the burden placed by their elaborate English orders on undertrained Hindustani-speaking staffs in little government offices, the insecurity of government workers, the sure knowledge that if dismissed they would find no other employment, the inability of the political system to give voice to peasants who would rather be silent than disagree with a coat-and-tie-attired government official—all this was bound to attract and promote a few Dr. Gopes. His thick glasses didn't help him; he saw and was aware of only what occurred within three feet of him, and he didn't remember that for more than a few minutes. That made it easy to resist his orders, to hope that he would forget them, to adjust—until one needed his help. Then, like Dr. Agarwal and Ram Sewak faced with threats from the auditors over the condom registers, you appreciated how much power this man had.

Ram Sewak and I called Dr. Gope "pagala" ("the lunatic"). His lunacy was little more than bad manners and an inability to make connections. Even when forced to absorb a new piece of information, he took it in as an isolated fact and refused to generalize from it. Each case of a midwife unable to convince village women to adopt family planning suggested to him that the midwife in question was lazy and not being sufficiently nagged by her superiors. Each failure of the jeep to arrive at the promised time showed that on a particular morning Dr. Gope, who kept the

162

keys, had been busy. Neither suggested anything about training, procedures, or putting things together.

But having written Dr. Gope off, I had to ask myself about the Peace Corps. How different was *its* response? True, it elevated the need to *hear* practically to the level of a sacrament. But was it hearing without listening?

Neither the Peace Corps nor Dr. Gope would try to compute the point at which so many parts of a machine are defective that a new one is needed. Neither knew how to make a fresh start, and so Dr. Gope until the very end, and the Peace Corps until almost the end, clung to the mechanic's remedial theory: find the rattle and fix it.

I had resolved not to bring any more rattles to Dr. Gope's attention; now, seeing the connection between his aimless questions and those of the Peace Corps, I resolved to ignore both of them.

In the heat, this seemed a pretty good solution.

16.

The mukhia had selected as groom an engineer at a steel mill. But much had to be done. B. P. took the train to Patna to arrange the lights, catering, and other services for the wedding. After dinner one evening, Judy and I decided to see for ourselves how the preparations in the Katriar house were going. In spite of the low humidity, there were few stars. We stumbled over odd bricks and stones, cursing the fact that no one replaced the lights outside the cold storage plant when they burned out. The courtyard was deserted. The back door of the mukhia's house was closed but not latched. I pushed it open and ducked under its low lintel. In the kitchen a small coal fire burned, a pile of chappatis before it, but no one was there. The lights of the main bedroom, at the opposite end of the courtyard, were burning. As we started towards them, I noticed a figure in the darkened portico on my right. It was Shobha. She was crying, her head buried in the folds of her white sari. Her sobbing could be heard over the hum of the lights.

"Shobha, what is it?" Judy asked.

Shobha lifted her head. Her sobs were louder. "The wedding. Everything. It's off, it's going to be in Patna, not Barhi. I won't be married here . . ." she looked around at the house, her world. "It's because of papa."

"Your father?" Judy asked.

"Don't you know? He had a heart attack in Patna two nights ago. The doctors say he can't travel back to Barhi. But he wants the wedding to go on anyway. He says it may be his last chance. So we'll all go to Patna tomorrow for the wedding."

164

Judy and I thought about the mukhia, not the wedding. So much had happened. Dr. Agarwal's son had died. Mrs. Srivastava had been abandoned by her husband. The Bengali had made a paper globe for his son while he grew to fear his neighbors. Ratna Chakraverty, one of the midwives and a friend of Judy's, had been driven to a nervous breakdown by the tensions of her lonely life, her affair with a married schoolteacher, the problems of her penniless family. Now the mukhia.

With the Katriars in Patna for the wedding, Judy and I fled the last weeks of the hot season by traveling to the mountains of Kashmir. We returned with the rains, prepared to stick it out for six months more, to prove that in a year and a half we had at least mastered the art of waiting.

But we would not be idle. Ram Sewak and I made up our minds to visit every major village in the block. Our first destination was a set of villages about ten miles from the Hazaribagh Road which had heretofore escaped our net. The bus carried us to Padma, where the Raja of Ramgarh had his old palace, and from there we fanned out, bumping over dirt roads, holding meetings, returning to Padma about four in the afternoon. There, while waiting for the bus to Barhi, we listened to the watchman who lived at the gate of the Raja's estate talk of the "good old days."

At the far end of the green tunnel of trees leading toward Hazaribagh a shaky red spot appeared and, as it drew nearer, assumed the form of a bus. "Is that an express bus, or a local?" I asked the watchman. He glanced at Ram Sewak's watch. "Local, Sahib. It stops here." Ram Sewak and I pushed our bikes across the road and stood beside an old woman carrying a basket of vegetables.

The bus stopped and the old woman pulled herself up the steps. The conductor leaned out and told Ram Sewak and me to get on. Ram Sewak pointed at our bikes and asked the conductor to come out and help us load them on the roof.

The conductor shook his head. "Sorry, no room on top. I can't take you." The driver shifted the bus loudly into low gear.

"Wait a minute, Driver Sahib," Ram Sewak called out. Conductor Sahib, there's lots of room on top, just give us a hand."

We had been through this so often that I firmly told the

conductor to stop making excuses and to load our cycles. He laughed merrily. "Sorry sahibs. I don't have the right kind of tickets for your bikes. Let's go, Driver Sahib."

The last time this happened I had sworn to conduct a one-man sit-down in front of the bus until our cycles were loaded. But I did nothing and the bus left.

Ram Sewak turned to me. "Well, Pope Sahib, shall we wait for the next bus or cycle in?"

"Do what you want. I'm going to catch that driver in Barhi, and I'm going to show him that passengers have rights too!" I jumped on my bike and pedaled wildly up the hill. It was ten miles from Padma to Barhi, quite hilly, and it was ninety-five degrees and muggy. At our normal sedate pace we took an hour to make the trip; the bus would take twenty minutes.

I hadn't decided what I would do when I arrived. The bus would be almost ready to leave Barhi by then. The driver might try to drive off when he saw me. I had splendid visions of throwing him and the conductor off the bus. Meanwhile I was straining to keep going, propelled only by my desire for vindication.

All the excuses that I had kept in reserve for moments like this vanished. I did not think that the system was to blame, that since you couldn't get mad every time something went wrong it was best not to get mad at all, that there might be a good reason for the unreasonable.

Chickens scatterd as I raced through the villages. I kept looking at my watch. Did I have time to unstrap my canteen and guzzle the tepid cup that remained? I had no choice. I had to. I slowed down, took the canteen in one hand, and I tried to pour water down my throat as I pedaled. Most of it ended up on my sweat-soaked shirt. I cursed my bad physical condition. The bus would escape. The driver and conductor, sensing me behind them, would cut short their stop in Barhi.

I was making better time on the downhill stretch, and as I got to the bridge at the bottom of the hill I could see the dust and smoke of the bazaar.

I couldn't keep up the pace. Energy and anger were largely spent. But at the crossing there were two buses. When I reached the concrete traffic island I could read the license plate of the one I was chasing, B393. I rode up to the flank of the bus and tossed my bike against a wall. I peered through the dirty windows. The driver's seat was empty, there was no conductor in the aisle. I had caught them!

I stopped to catch my breath. My shirt was a runny red from the dust of the road and sweat. People gathered around to see what had brought me gasping into the bazaar. "What is it, Sahib? What has happened?"

My Hindi came slowly, I told my story briefly. Onlookers nodded. "Yes, they're scoundrels, those conductors. They think they own the buses!"

I was tired, but the confrontation I wanted was developing. I had the sympathetic onlookers, now for the villain. The conductor approached the bus, chatting with the Barhi dispatcher. He had not yet seen me, he was not even thinking about me. I elbowed my way through the crowd and planted myself in front of them. The dispatcher looked up. I stood in their way. The conductor did not recognize me at first, then he looked puzzled. What did I want with him now? I had planned to get off at Barhi, and now I was there.

"I have a complaint, Dispatcher Sahib. This man refused to load our cycles at Padma, even after he stopped for passengers. I want action taken."

The dispatcher looked down at his record book and casually asked the conductor, "Why didn't you take them on?"

The conductor mumbled that he had not understood where we were going, had been late, had been crowded. The dispatcher expected this would satisfy me.

I was breathing too heavily to shout, so I tried to sound menacing. "That's no answer. I want him to sign a statement *now*, saying that he refused to pick us up. I want no claims when his case comes up that it was some other driver, some other day, some other bus."

The dispatcher sighed.

"I won't let this bus leave!" I warned. "I should have stopped it at Padma, and if I have to I'll stop it now!"

The dispatcher was uncomfortable. He had never seen me in this mood and was divided between his loyalty to the conductor and his insecurity about the raving sahib. He assured me that he had heard the conductor's confession and would testify at the hearing to what I claimed. I could come with him that instant and fill out my complaint. Would I like to come with him?

My bluff had failed. I would walk off with the dispatcher, fill in and certify the forms, mail them, and wait. The gesture I demanded could not be extracted; I had taken the first step into a bureaucratic labyrinth. The only way I could have won was to have caught the man climbing off the bus and hit him. And then all I would have won would have been a clean end to my anger, and remorse.

This mad chase was a sign that I was losing patience with the limits I had put on myself in Barhi. Chasing the bus made no sense as a means of insuring that we would catch the next one. The Barhi State Bus Company was protected from my indignation by layers of clerks, forms, and official procedures. I had chased the bus because I wanted to lay claim to an individual worth that was incomprehensible in Barhi. Ram Sewak and I were "passengers," and one of the duties of a passenger is to put up with bad service. Shaking my fist in the bazaar, I had become to those around me something different, a "furious sahib," and had received the deference and the runaround that are due an angry white man. I thought that the dispatcher's response should reflect not only my behavior in the bazaar but also the humiliation of being left behind by a bus, and the pain and sweat of the chase. The dispatcher did not, could not, see the connection. Neither could anyone else. I had become unpredictable.

I had tried to avoid this. From the beginning of our stay, Barhi could easily have put us in a separate compartment of its mind labeled "Americans" and forgotten us. Most of Barhi did, having decided that our heads were constructed differently. But I had hoped that a few people would see that Judy and I had not different ways, but a different way. I thought there was a connection between our effort to know Jagdish, our refusal to bribe officials, our relative dedication to a full four-hour day of work, and our impatience with bad service on buses. Barhi wanted to pick and choose, to attach a thousand labels to my thousand and one oddities, and to sum up the contradictions in the term "sahib."

In fact, much of what I did was contradictory. I paid Jagdish twice the going wage and haggled with him over pennies on the grocery bill. I accepted the hospitality of the Katriars but rejected the paternalism. I loaned money to B. P. Katriar and refused to loan it to Girja, the driver of the jeep. So most of

Barhi wrote us off as "inscrutable." Their explanation was that we were from a cold climate.

Ram Sewak had to go deeper. Although he saw the paradoxes, he also saw that they disturbed us, that we were not at ease with ourselves. He was able to understand that what I wanted was not to act as I would in America, but in a way that would illustrate, to Barhi, certain things about myself, my attitudes, my history. He understood this because he was a phenomenal translator. Jagdish responded to it because he was remarkably open. But even they were able to react only because I did some translating of my own and tried to keep a layer of India between us.

Now I had shaken that layer off. I had made choices without thinking, "What will this say to people, how will they understand it?" I had grabbed for an emotional brass ring and had missed it.

"What the hell am I doing chasing a bus?" was that day's version of "What the hell am I doing here?" The new phrasing alarmed me; it could just as easily have come out as a variant of the question I did not want to answer, "What the hell am I doing wrong?"

At the hospital one morning soon after the wild bus chase, we arrived to find a deep, troubling silence. No one flirted with the nurses, no one joked in the pharmaceutical room. "What has happened?" Judy asked the group. We had long since given up asking anyone in particular.

Dr. Agarwal looked up, and Dr. Agarwal *never* looked up from his prescription pad while he worked.

"Panditji had cholera. He collapsed last night but they did not call me until morning. He's very sick. I've been giving him fluids, but he doesn't respond."

Panditji was the hospital watchman, a wizened Brahmin with a sharp nose, a high, bald forehead, and a high voice. He hopped about answering the summons of the staff or opening doors, little white tufts of hair behind his ears bouncing up and down. I had not liked him. He had a wretched job but too obviously considered it wretched not because he was a man but because he was a Brahmin.

But neither his birth nor my feelings were relevant that morning. Death, or the threat of it were nothing new in the dispensary. Most of the patients who were brought to the small ward were too sick to live. Their families came and stayed with them, the staff nursed and cared for them to the limit of its skill and facilities, always with calm and dignity. The mourning after a death spoke of the value of the life which had just ended and transformed what might have been personal and frightening into a ritual.

But Panditji was one of the staff; when cholera struck him its impact was not confined to the ward with its small knot of white-robed visitors around a bed, its smooth concrete floor and symmetrical double doors. The staff went in to speak to Panditji's wife and when they came out the fear came with them. Dr. Agarwal sagged as the day diminished, finally abandoning the dispensary office and moving his chair and examination instruments to his front porch. When Judy and I came back from a lunch which we had not eaten he was hunched over the table, re-reading his medical manuals and jotting down notes. Pandit's wife had left; the quiet ward seemed to say that death had won.

Dr. Agarwal refused to give in. He continued intravenous fluids and drugs. Pandit passed into a coma. About seven in the evening he died, and as the staff lifted him into the jeep for the journey home to his village and family, Dr. Agarwal began to talk about Pandit.

"We should never lose a cholera case, not if we are called in time. They were late, but still I should have been able to save him. But he had no resistance at all, no strength." He turned to me. "Did you know he was only forty-five?"

"What?" I asked, incredulous. "He looked like an old man!"

"It was diet. He would only eat rice, it was a prestige food; he was a Brahmin. During the height of the famine, when my family, Mr. Kumar, the Katriars, all were eating wheat and millet, Pandit ate rice. On his salary that meant he ate nothing else, and often little rice. He starved himself to death during the famine. That's when he aged, during the hard times. He didn't have to." Dr. Agarwal shrugged helplessly and stepped out into the night.

The next day Judy told me she wanted to leave India. She was oppressed by Pandit's death, it was an omen. It took several weeks of argument, quarrels, and tears before she overcame my stubborn intention to stay. At first I was afraid of Ram Sewak's reaction. Privately, without telling Judy, I tested him. I told him we might leave, that Dr. Gope's interference had made our work impossible, that I was no longer useful either to Dr. Agarwal or to him. The sensible course was for Judy and me to return to the States and for Ram Sewak and Dr. Agarwal to get their longed-for transfers.

Ram Sewak was not shocked. He thought he could get a transfer in a month or two. I was not that confident, but his answer lightened my spirits. If he could get a transfer, then we would both be leaving Barhi. It would not be so bad.

The monsoon that second year never came. I searched the circle of great white clouds for one that would mean rain, but the sprouts and weeds of the first monsoon weeks turned brown and died. The rice seedlings remained in their nurseries, becoming ragged and frayed as their roots set. Half-plowed fields dried out and cracked. Only the fresh green sisum leaves showed that it was August.

I worried about the crops, but mainly to take my mind off my loss of heart. We did less work and got others to do less. I discovered that the jeep had not gone to Hazaribagh for repairs. Well, there was no gas money if the jeep were repaired. Nevertheless, I swore at Girja over the incident. Ram Sewak watched gravely.

The mukhia's health improved slowly after the wedding. I had resented his paternalism, his haughty claims of dedication to the public good, his politics. But he had been, until the heart attack, one of the few people in Barhi with vitality and integrity, a man who bent but was not broken by the impotence around him. And because he had appropriated the place of father, even against my will, I felt a mixed love for him.

As the hot August dragged on without enough rain, with frustrations that were no different from those that we had met the first months in Barhi, I began to look forward to our departure.

After another threat from Dr. Gope that if Ram Sewak did not meet his target he would be fired, I told Judy we would leave as soon as it could be arranged.

Ram Sewak did what he could to obtain his transfer. He spent most of each day with us. Ostensibly he was looking for things in our discard pile that he might want to buy, but it was more than that. He invited us to eat with him. We sat for hours talking about what I would do in the States, what he would do after his transfer, what we had done or failed to do in our year together.

When we told the mukhia we had set the first of September as the date for leaving, he pulled himself up long enough to snort. "What did I tell you, Mr. Pope, the first day you came? I said you would fail! I warned you!" He seemed more amused at having his prophecy fulfilled than sad at losing his adopted children. The rest of the family were more emotional, but as Judy said, "People never really believed that we would stay or that we would leave. If we had left in December, on schedule, they would have said, 'What, you're leaving?' And once we leave, we won't exist for most of them."

We went searching for Dr. Agarwal to tell him the news and found him with Mr. Kumar, Madan Babu, and the headmaster of the high school. We waited while the servants scurried around for chairs. I sat down heavily and looked to Judy for help. She was looking to me.

Without any preparation I blurted out in Hindi, "Well, we're leaving."

"Another vacation?" he asked routinely. "Where is it this time?"

"No, we're going back to the States, leaving Barhi, quitting!"

I never expected what happened. Dr. Agarwal, who had been leaning forward to sip his drink, fell back into his chair. His face showed the first honest surprise I had ever seen on it. We wiped his brow. "That's . . . quite a shock," he managed to mumble, "quite a shock."

Then our feelings came out in a rush. Judy broke in, "It doesn't make sense any more. Dr. Gope makes the whole thing impossible. All Carl and I do is attract his attention and make life miserable for you and Ram Sewak. We're leaving so you can get your transfers quickly and get away from that vicious old man!" We had never before attacked any Indian in this fashion.

Dr. Agarwal, unable to break his habits, looked to me for the definitive word. But Judy had said it and all I added was, "We're sorry. We can't take it any longer."

No one spoke, waiting for the doctor to give a cue. "Well," he said, struggling for compliments, "as long as you were here we had someone reliable. I could give an assignment and trust you to carry it out."

Judy smiled. It was his usual praise for departing staff.

"When are you going?"

"In about a week, as soon as we can pack."

"We'll give you the jeep to take your trunks to the train station," he said decisively, glad to be back on the familiar ground of command. "That way you won't have to worry about missing the train."

"You'll have to come eat with me again, Mr. Pope," Madan Babu broke in with his distinctive Punjabi English. "You must take back the memory of good Punjabi food."

"Come have chicken, one more time," said Mr. Kumar, laughing. "You managed your transfer before any of us!"

"Well," I mumbled, "we'd better go. Thanks for the invitations, we're going to miss you." And we left.

Back at the house, we stared at the whitewashed walls.

"What's first?" I said to Judy.

"Sort out the trunks." She sounded hoarse.

Jagdish made only two or three meals that week. People who had not previously invited us to dinner rushed to have the sahibs over before they left. Any meal that we were free, Ram Sewak would preempt. People hailed us on the road, asking if we were leaving and saying goodbye. An old Muslim woman stopped us to bestow a toothless blessing. Ram Jan Maulwi rubbed his fingers together and laughed, "Write, eh?"

The pile of goods we would not take with us diminished rapidly as gifts, especially to Jagdish and the family next door. When we had finished packing Jagdish brought a rickshaw and loaded it with all the junk we had neither sold nor given away. We could not imagine what he would do with it, but the mukhia pointed out that if Jagdish had hired a rickshaw to haul it he had a use for it.

The day before we left Jagdish came into the dining room where Judy and I were sorting through our papers. He stood in the middle of the floor, hands clasped behind his back. He looked down, furrowed his brow, and like a student practicing a recitation said, " We will be sad when you leave. It was good working for you. Especially because we never fought. If I made a mistake, you told me, and I didn't repeat it. No bickering. And

you were always ready with help and good advice for poor
people like us. Please write when you return to your own company. *And morning, sir, and birkpast?*"

It was the English phrase he had used about breakfast for
eighteen months.

"Jagdish," I said as he turned to leave the room, "you really
are a first-class *pukka* cook."

"Do you think you can find a job soon?" I asked Jagdish.

"I'll try. I hear there's an opening at a rest house near Jhumri
Tilaiya."

I told him I would write a recommendation and gave him our
transistor radio as a parting gift. One of my more irrational acts
of stinginess had been to refuse him permission to take the radio
home at night. I had, unbelievably, been trying to save the bat-
teries.

I would miss Barhi. The dining-room table with its faded
checked tablecloth, the bazaar lined with symbols of projects
that had not been accomplished, the bench in front of the tea
stall where I waited with Ram Sewak for buses that didn't come,
the coal yard where I met an orange-robed Hindu holy man to
supply him with condoms, the blank walls where I had hung
family planning posters. I rolled a bit of grit between my fingers,
watched the lizards copulating amidst the bamboo supports of
the roof. Judy rested her hand against my neck. "I'm sorry," she
said, "we just weren't lucky."

We had reservations, first-class this time, on the night train to
Delhi. Ram Sewak and the hospital staff loaded the jeep and
drove us to the station. The staff and jeep went on to the cinema.
Ram Sewak was going to wait with us for the train. But the train
did not come. We gossiped. It was two hours after train time. The
sign at the dispatcher's window had indicated that the train was
one-half hour late and had not left Gaya Station. Now it was two
and one-half hours late, still at Gaya.

Finally we persuaded Ram Sewak to leave. He said goodbye
and walked down the dusty dark platform, his white dhoti swinging in the breeze, his heavy sandals falling one before the other,
the lights shining off his oiled black hair. I felt like crying.

In Delhi we had lunch with Sneh Bhalla, a tall, elegant
Punjabi who had been a language instructor in Peace Corps train-

174

ing. She had returned to India and was doing a nutrition survey. She took us to the cafeteria on the roof where we ate under an awning. Beyond, the barren domes of the tombs of the Lodi emperors stood in a now desolate garden. The dust of early September obscured the rest of the city.

We heaped yogurt and cucumbers, spiced lentils, flat chappatis, rice and vegetable curries on our plates, and dug into our last meal in India while Sneh described her job. The survey was to be used in villages around Delhi to assess the diet. But the raw data coming in had no value. The work was not going well.

"It's difficult to do this from a desk," Sneh told us. "How can I take account of how things may be in the villages? I have never been in a village." She smiled ironically. "I don't really know why I have never gone to the villages. Now if I suggest it they all tell me, 'Oh, no, most unsuited for a woman.' Yet half the people in the villages are women."

We finished eating. Even Sneh, whom I respected for her strength, had stayed on one side of the barrier between the new and the old India. I wondered why. Unlike Dr. Agarwal, she was at home in the new and had genuinely freed herself from those things in India's past, like caste and purdah, that her mind could not accept. She lived in India and not simply as India's guest, as Judy and I had. Where Jagdish was simple and unformed, she was sophisticated and mature. Where Ram Sewak lived by a kindness and competence that were so personal that he never expected to encounter them in anyone else, Sneh offered a choice that anyone might perceive. Two generations ago her family had left a village in the Punjab where women wore baggy pants and tunics and giggled when asked the name of their husbands. What had been done in two generations by her family others might do in one. Yet Sneh was unable to offer this choice to peasant women. She could not do what Judy and I had tried to do.

But what had we done? To what purpose had I worn khadi? We had lived in Barhi, but we had not lived off Barhi. The checks from the embassy in Delhi, the plane fare back to the States, the vacations in the South, the Peace Corps doctor in Calcutta all came as we did, from the United States.

We had resided in Barhi as sahibs. Our small house had become The Big House. The Peace Corps had arranged this, instructing us to work within the bureaucracy, to be saluted as

"Oh, Governor" by the old women in the bazaar, giving us generous travel allowances and putting us in Barhi where only the rich travel. The Peace Corps had guarded us from the vagaries of Barhi medicine, Barhi diet, Barhi newspapers, and a Bihari future. It had tied us to the betel-stained courtyard of the New Secretariat in Patna and to the marble American Embassy in Delhi.

Then, with the same insensitivity to roles and connections that marked Dr. Gope, it clung to its touching faith that we were free agents, writing on clean slates. Could it have believed otherwise?

We ended our tour in India inside the fence of British India with its bougainvillea hedges and ordered gardens. Here, at the Indian International Center where Sneh worked, the flowering shrubs and hedges were more ornate than those of the Dak Bungalow in Barhi. But I remembered those first days in the bungalow. I thought of the fence around it, of the goats that jumped it, of my fears of what lay outside. Now, looking at Judy and Sneh, I knew that my first fears had betrayed me. It was not that the fence had failed to shut out India; I had let it shut me in.